creative
scarves

20+ stylish projects to craft and stitch

Tiffany Windsor
Heidi Borchers
Savannah Starr

Fons&Porter
CINCINNATI, OHIO

contents

 # introduction

A quick online search gives a detailed look at the rich history of the scarf from Ancient Rome and Egypt through its emergence from function to fashion accessory by the early nineteenth century. Fast-forward to today, and scarves have now become an everyday accessory for all seasons, the perfect finishing touch to just about any outfit.

What sets a scarf apart as your own fashion statement is the ability to personalize it with your own creative touches. In designing this collection of scarves, we have focused on sharing creative techniques that the beginning hand-crafter can easily follow and that the hands-on craft enthusiast can build upon and personalize for one-of-a-kind results.

As fourth and sixth generation crafters, we have grown up in a very creative environment and have definitely lost count of the number of projects we have created for business and pleasure over the years. We grew up in a crafty space where everything was glued, so we enthusiastically embraced the creation of this collection where we could combine our sewing, stitching and crafty talents to create scarves for all seasons and occasions.

Our joy in designing and creating this scarf collection together is celebrating each generation's style, colors and trends, and teaching each other new techniques. We browsed fabric and thrift stores to find just the right fabrics to use and deconstruct; we tested glues, dyes, paints and inks; we dipped into our own creative supplies for yarn, beads, rhinestones, charms and other embellishments. We all agree that this collection—from the simplicity of subtle design to the enticing detail of couture—is by far the most fun we have had creating and wearing! We hope you in turn are inspired to make and enjoy these scarves for every season, and that they lead to further creativity on your own.

tools & materials

Let's go over some of the main materials and tools you will need to complete the projects. Later in this section is a complete checklist of everything you will want to have on hand.

Fabric

For those who enjoy hand-sewing or using their sewing machines to stitch a scarf, there is a huge variety of suitable fabrics for scarf making available at your local fabric store. Once you decide how you want to embellish or decorate your scarf, you can select from soft and smooth to patterned, textured and bulky fabrics. Keep in mind how the fabric will feel wrapped around your neck. Will it drape nicely? Will it be easy to hem? Will it wash and dry?

Readymade scarves

Another great option for your base scarf is to select a readymade scarf. Since scarves are a fashion basic, you can find selections in many colors, finishes, shapes and sizes. When you want to customize a readymade scarf, you can find excellent online sources for plain white scarves in natural fibers that are ready for dyeing. Choices include silk, cotton and rayon, bamboo rayon, velvets and more. When dyeing your own fabrics, you must select a 100-percent natural fiber such as cotton, rayon, linen or wool. The benefit of readymade scarves is that you do not need to finish the edges or hem the fabric. Ready-made scarves can be found in traditional square and rectangular shapes along with shawls, sarongs and bandannas. They can be gathered, spiraled, fringed, seamless, circular and more.

Yarn and wool

Whether using it to create an entire scarf or for fringe or embellishments, yarn is very versatile. You can select from many different weights including super-fine, fine, light, medium, bulky, super-bulky and more. Whenever possible, you will want to feel the yarn you are considering using to select the softest finishes. Affordable yarns can be purchased by the skein at your local craft store. Custom-spun and dyed yarns can be found at specialty shops.

Wool roving is a piece of wool that has been combed, drawn into a clump and then twisted slightly to hold the fibers (see Resources sidebar in the back of the book). It is used in a wet-felting technique to make the Felted Fantasy Scarflet in Chapter 5.

Beads

When using beads to embellish the ends of yarn fringe, be sure to select large-hole beads. Bulky yarns need plenty of room to pass through the bead opening. Beads with smaller holes can be used for bead drops and hand-beading work.

Dyes

There are many different choices when selecting dyes to color your own scarves and fabrics. There are dyes that require soda ash, salt, heat, and other specific materials and methods to set the dyes permanently into your fabrics. Sometimes we select a dye for its ease of use, other times because we have used it before or we know we want a very specific color that is available from only one supplier. Keep in mind that dye reacts differently with different fabric blends.

Some manufacturers recommend dyeing fabrics in the washing machine; others suggest buckets. Whichever dyeing method you select, we recommend that you test, test, test. When testing a new dye or dyeing method, we often cut one scarf into several smaller pieces so we can test the application. Sometimes we don't end up with the color we had in mind for a specific project, but we still end up with beautiful fabric samples we can use for other projects.

Paints and inks

There are many different choices for fabric paints, but the most important quality is leaving the fabric as soft as possible while getting an intense opaque

Old shirts or thrift-store buys can find new life in an upcycled scarf project.

When yarn is required for a project, be sure to select the softest finishes for maximum comfort.

or semiopaque color. You will want to make your selection depending on how you are applying your paint to the fabric. Applications include stenciling, hand-painting, block printing and more. Some paints may need to be heat-set to become permanent; always follow the manufacturer's instructions.

Some stamping, printing and painting techniques require longer open (or working) time, which means that the inks/paints take longer to dry. Screen printing inks and block printing inks can be used for these applications.

Paint palettes and brushes

Many different types of professional paint palettes can be used to hold and mix paint, but our crafty choices include nonstick mats, wax paper, freezer paper and paper plates.

Our crafty toolbox brushes always include a fine liner, a small round and several sizes of soft-bristle flats. Synthetic bristle can be used for these projects, and many of these brushes are easy to purchase in sets.

Stencils

Stencils are an easy way to add personalized designs to create one-of-a-kind scarves. From simple lettering to intricate laser-cut designs, stencils give the crafter the ability to add painted designs to many surfaces. Specialty applicators such as bristle brushes and pouncers are available for use with stencils, but we prefer to use cosmetic wedge sponges to apply paint on stencils.

Needles

When working with bulky yarns, plastic upholstery needles are a great choice. They are easy to thread, easy to hold, and when using them with netting, they glide smoothly through. When selecting smaller needles, keep in mind that embroidery threads require a needle with a larger eye while still being able to slip back through small bead holes.

Scissors and rotary cutters

It is important to use top-quality scissors, especially when cutting fabrics. If you do not already have a pair of scissors specially designated for fabrics in your craft tool box, be sure to add them soon! There is nothing worse than having thick or thin fabrics snag on overused scissors. We label our scissors that are specifically reserved for fabric. Then we won't be tempted to cut a piece of wire with them! When using the craft adhesive sheets and tapes, we recommend nonstick scissors.

Just as important as scissors, a top-quality rotary cutter and a self-healing cutting mat are excellent tools for any craft studio. Take great care when using rotary cutters because they are, of course, very sharp, and when used according to their package instructions, they can be very useful in cutting straight edges and multiple layers of fabric.

Glues and adhesives

Whenever we call out a specific glue in a project materials list, it is because we have tested glues to find out which will give you the best results every time. This becomes particularly important when you are working with craft foam (very difficult to glue!), using a washable dry adhesive, and even when you are applying dabs of glue to secure knots in your projects. Our go-to glues are Aleene's Original Tacky Glue, E-6000 and Aleene's Fabric Fusion Peel & Stick Sheets and Peel & Stick Tape.

Blue painter's tape is excellent for holding stencils in place on low-pile fabrics or for holding patterns in place on your work surface.

Toothpicks and wooden skewers

These handy, inexpensive applicators are a must whenever you are applying dabs of glue. We like to pour a small puddle of glue on a nonstick surface—just enough for a project—and then recap our glues. By replacing the cap quickly, you can preserve your glues for longer shelf life. A toothpick or skewer is

7

an easy way to apply a dab, dollop or a generous amount of glue to any surface.

Wet wipes

These are a must-have in any creative studio! Keeping your tools and hands clean while working with fabrics and yarns is a must.

Foamboard

Whenever we are creating our own stamps, we use foamboard to hold our craft foam shapes. You can create lots of stamps from one sheet of foamboard. We have used expensive foamboard for many projects but find that board from the discount store also works quite well. Foamboard is also very useful for laying out and pinning your materials in place.

supplies you will need

Here is a comprehensive list of all the materials, items and tools you will need to complete every scarf project in this book. For more specific details including types, amounts, sizes and colors, see the individual projects.

- Readymade scarves: rayon, silk (ombre-dyed), infinity-style knit, gauze, smooth finish (summer weight), black rayon (fringed)

- T-shirts, white hoodie sweatshirt with drawstring tie, flannel shirts, rayon dresses, knit top or dress, silk tops

- Fabric: bamboo rayon, textured poly silk, smooth gauze, organdy, velvet, Silkessence polyester, fleece, premium felt

- Yarn, merino wool roving, nylon netting, bridal-style netting with large open weave, mohair locks, silk gauze, and assorted others

- Crocheted doilies (including table runner/placemat sizes, etc.)

- Thread (including cotton crochet), embroidery floss, metallic embroidery thread

- Readymade felted flowers, large decorative buttons, large metal charm, sequins, beads, rhinestones

- Large metal ring with jump ring added, rondelles, end caps, eye pins, flat-head pins, lobster claw (optional)

- Fabric dye, fabric paint, Jacquard Textile Colors, acrylic paint, Speedball Screen Printing Ink, block printing ink (and foam tray), nail polish

- Rubber stamp (must be bold rubber stamp design mounted on wood block)

- Foamboard, craft foam sheet, self-adhesive craft foam alphabet letters, foam pool noodle

- Linoleum block, 5" × 7" (13cm × 18cm)

- Block cutters with tips of your choice

- Aleene's Fabric Fusion Permanent Fabric Adhesive, Peel & Stick Sheets and Peel & Stick Tape; OK To Wash-It (glue); Aleene's Original Tacky Glue; E-6000 glue

- Crochet hook, large plastic needle, sewing and embroidery needles

- Jewelry pliers: flat-head and round-nose

- Sewing machine, pom-pom maker, iron (preferably without steam holes), ironing board, straight pins

- No. 2 pencil, pens, chalk, black permanent marker (medium tip), large marking pen, gel bleach pen, .01 and .05 Sakura Pigma Micron pens

- Soft-bristle brushes: small round and ½" (13mm) flat

- Scissors, nonstick scissors, craft knife, rotary cutter, cutting mat, brayer

- Measuring cup(s) and spoons, 3 buckets, 2 plastic tubs

- Measuring tape, ruler

- Protective gloves

- Blue painter's tape, transparent tape, 3 ties (use knee-high nylon stockings or strips of spandex)

- Cosmetic sponges (wedge shape)

- Jar/can lids (various sizes), soft brush (optional), wax paper, paper plates, dish soap, white vinegar, spray bottle, water

- Paper towels, bath towel, wet wipes, sponge

- Bubble wrap, plain newsprint or packing paper, cardboard tube (from gift wrap)

- Wooden skewers or toothpicks

- Clear shrink plastic sheet (or other clear rigid plastic), white photocopy paper

- Patterns and stencils (see individual projects)

- 6' (1.8m) table (or a clean floor)

favorite ways to wear

Scarves are worn to provide warmth and comfort or worn as a featured fashion accessory. Whether simply looped or fancily twisted, a scarf allows you to add color, design and texture to any outfit.

There are dozens of ways to tie your scarves, and your choice will depend on the size and shape and how bulky you want the scarf to feel and hang.

When not being worn, there are lots of fun ways to store your scarves including specialty hangers, shower curtain rings, shoe organizers, coat hooks, clothespins and more. Some people even like to display their scarves as wall art!

When caring for your scarves, keep in mind: handmade, hand-wash. Use a mild soap and hang or lay out your scarves to dry. Most scarves can also be pressed with a slightly warm iron.

Infinity

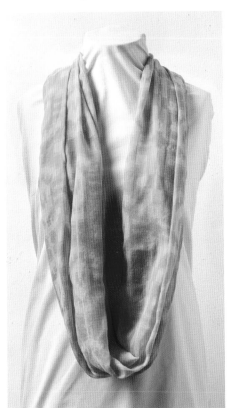

long loop

1 Tie scarf ends together to create a loop (if not an infinity-style scarf) and hang the loop around your neck, with the knot in the back.

2 For a layered look that is close to the neck, twist and loop the scarf around your neck once more.

short layered loops

Classic loop

1 Lay the scarf around the back of your neck, letting one-third of it hang in front of 1 shoulder.

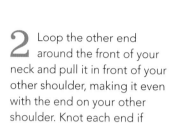

2 Loop the other end around the front of your neck and pull it in front of your other shoulder, making it even with the end on your other shoulder. Knot each end if desired.

Classic loop with tied ends

Slipknot

1 Fold the scarf in half lengthwise and drape it around the back of your neck.

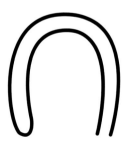

2 Pull both ends through the loop and adjust the tightness and the position of the knot as desired.

Ascot style

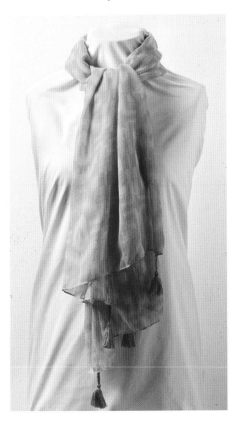

1 Lay the scarf around the back of your neck, letting it hang slightly longer on 1 side.

2 Fold the longer end over the other twice.

3 Bring the end up through the loop at your neck. Spread the top (front) layer of the scarf to cover the layer beneath.

Hidden knot

1 Lay the scarf around the back of your neck, letting it hang slightly longer on 1 side.

2 Loop the scarf around your neck in the classic loop style shown earlier in this section.

3 Tie the scarf ends into a knot near the loop. Adjust and fluff the loop as needed to hide the knot.

European loop

1 Fold the scarf in half lengthwise and drape it around the back of your neck.

2 Pull 1 end under and through the loop.

3 Pull the other end over and through the loop, then tighten and adjust as needed.

Loose drape

1 Loop the scarf around your neck in the classic loop style shown earlier in this section, only with 1 end shorter than the other.

2 Take the longer end and pull it up and across your neck, tucking it into the loops on the opposite shoulder. Arrange the draped fabric as needed.

Lots of knots

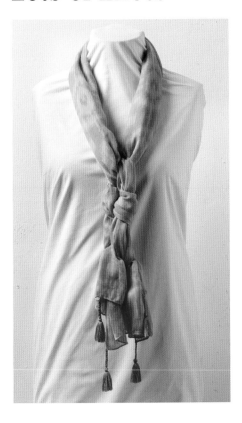

1 Lay the scarf around the back of your neck.

2 Tie a knot in the middle of the scarf.

3 Leave some space, then tie another knot below the first. Repeat tying as many knots as you can.

Twist

1 Loop the scarf around your neck in the classic loop style shown earlier in this section.

2 Begin twisting 1 scarf end several times around the loop toward the center front.

3 Repeat step 2 for the other scarf end, ending at the center front. Adjust as needed.

1
spring

Ombre-Dyed Crochet Doilies

by Tiffany Windsor

When you first think of doilies, you might envision vintage home décor accents. Think again! With a fresh splash of color combined in a mix-and-match style, doilies can be easily transformed into a stylish scarf.

materials

- Crochet doilies, including table runners, placemats and other shapes (if dyeing, 100-percent cotton is best)

- Cotton crochet thread and crochet hook (or needle and matching thread)

- Dye (read package instructions for additional materials needed for your specific dye)

- Buckets (3 for ombre effect)

- Measuring cup(s)

- Measuring spoons (for dye)

- Protective gloves

- Scissors

- Iron

How to join pieces using whip stitch or slip stitch

To whip stitch

To whip stitch 2 pieces together using a sewing needle and thread, first place the pieces right sides together. Working from back to front, pass your threaded needle under and through the back (inner) loops of each piece, then pull it over the front to the next set of back loops and continue stitching. Knot and tie off to finish.

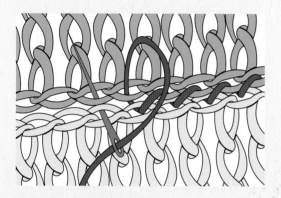

To slip stitch

To slip stitch 2 pieces together using a crochet hook and yarn, place the pieces right sides together and begin with your yarn in a slipknot on the hook. Insert the hook through the back (inner) loop of each piece, yarn over, and pull back through both loops and the loop on the hook. Continue, then tie off and trim.

Start with the joining yarn in a slipknot on your hook.

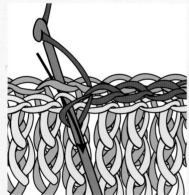

1 Lay out, join and wash

Lay out your doilies until you achieve the design, length and width of the scarf you desire. With needle and thread (or crochet thread), stitch them together using a simple whip stitch. If you have crochet skills, you can also join doily to doily with a crochet hook and slip stitch. (See sidebar "How to join pieces using whip stitch or slip stitch.")

Wash your joined doily scarf. You do not need to put it into the dryer because you will want the threads to be wet when dyeing.

2 Ombre-dye the scarf

Prepare the first dye bath with 1½ gallons (5.7L) of water, and mix dye to the darkest hue. In the second bucket add 6 cups (1.4L) of water and 2 cups (0.5L) of dye (from the first bath). In the third bucket, add 6 cups (1.4L) of water and a ½ cup (118ml) of dye (from the first bath). This will give you 3 hues of the same color for the ombre effect.

Put on protective gloves. Following the dye package instructions, place the entire scarf into the lightest bath for the suggested length of time. Remove from the bath and dip the ends 14" to 16" (36cm to 41cm) into the medium bath for the suggested time. You should be able to drape the excess doily fabric over the side of the bucket while the tips remain in the dye bath. Remove from the bath and dip the ends (about 6" [15cm]) into the dark bath for the suggested time.

3 Wash, dry and iron
Once the scarf is dyed to your liking, wash and dry all pieces according to the dye package instructions. Iron and wear! For the scarf shown, a single table runner was used for the main body of the scarf with 3 small doilies stitched onto each end.

hints and tips

✿ Scour your local thrift stores for doilies of all shapes and sizes. Keep in mind that traditional single doilies can be combined to create beautiful patterns, but keep your eyes open for table runners, placemats and other intriguing shapes.

✿ Don't worry if the doilies are in disrepair because you can easily add new doilies to fill in holes, mend the doilies with needle and thread, or grab your crochet hook and cotton crochet thread to make repairs.

✿ Keep in mind when dyeing your doilies that depending on the cotton content and the base color of the threads, each doily

may take on a color of its own. If you want all the pieces to color match exactly, you need to start with all the doilies made from the same colored cotton thread.

✿ If you have poly-cotton blends, the dye will appear more variegated as most dyes will not dye the polyester threads.

✿ While you are dyeing the scarf, be sure to drop additional doilies and the crochet thread into the dye baths so that you have additional matching pieces and thread to use to further decorate your scarf. Depending on the type of dye you use, you need to follow package instructions to set the dye for permanency.

Layered Squares

by Tiffany Windsor

Inspired by quilting squares, this project takes on a charming, tattered look from ripped fabrics. The soft floral tones reflect the colors of spring. The geometric look is repeated within the design with round and square sequins and iridescent beads.

materials

- Fabric for scarf, 2⅛ yards (1.9m) (shown is a lightweight textured poly silk); finished size 15" × 76" (38cm × 193cm)*

- 3 colors of fabric (lightweight smooth gauze) for torn squares and fringe

  Colors/amounts used for the scarf shown, all yardage 44" (112cm) wide:
  Dark rose, ½ yard (0.5m)**
  Light green, ¼ yard (0.25m)**
  Light rose, ¼ yard (0.25m)**

- 56 sequins—a mixture of black square, white round and pink iridescent round

- 280 iridescent beads, ⅛"(3mm)

- Aleene's Fabric Fusion Permanent Fabric Adhesive or fabric glue

- Measuring tape

- Scissors

- Iron (optional)

- Needle and thread

- Wax paper

- Wooden skewer or toothpick (for applying glue)

- Sewing machine (optional)

*You can make several scarves with this amount of fabric. Add additional inches/centimeters to width to create ripped edges.

**Allow for extra when ripping (versus cutting).

1 Start the tattered edge

For the tattered edge effect, measure approximately ½" (13mm) from the scarf fabric selvedge and cut down approximately 2" (5cm) with scissors. Measure across 16" (41cm) and repeat by cutting down about 2" (5cm) with scissors.

2 Finish the edge

Starting at the first cut, use both hands to rip the fabric apart. Repeat at the second cut. This will give both sides of your scarf fabric a tattered edge.

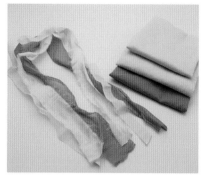

3 Make strips

To create the squares/rectangles, first measure and mark the dark rose fabric at 2½" (6cm) intervals. Snip and rip 5 strips. Measure and mark the light green fabric at approximately 1¾" (4.4cm) intervals. Snip and rip 7 strips. Measure and cut the light rose fabric at approximately 1½" (4cm) intervals. Snip and rip 6 strips. (The remaining yardage will be used to snip and rip the fringe.) If desired, you can iron each piece flat at this point or leave them curled at the edges.)

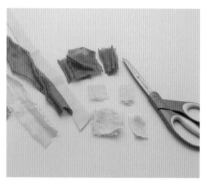

4 Cut fabric into pieces

Cut the dark rose fabric strips into forty-two 2" (5cm) lengths (each piece now measures 2" × 2½" [5cm × 6cm]). Cut 14 of these pieces in half to measure 2½" × 1" (6cm × 3cm). You should now have 28 full and 28 half-cut pieces of dark rose.

Cut the light green fabric strips into fifty-six 1½" (4cm) lengths (each piece now measures 1½" × 1¾" [4cm × 4.4cm]). Cut the light rose fabric strips into fifty-six 1" (3cm) lengths (each piece now measures 1" × 1½" [3cm × 4cm]). Cut pieces in half when needed to layer over the smaller dark rose pieces.

5 Create the fringe strips

Measure and repeat the ripping technique to create approximately ½" (13mm) strips of colored fabric for the fringe. You will notice that these narrow strips of torn fabrics curl a lot along the edges.

6 Assemble the layered fabrics

Create each stack by layering the dark rose, light green and light rose pieces. Select a sequin and place it in the center. Use needle and thread to stitch and knot the sequin and a bead in place in the center of the layered fabric. The thread is knotted at the top of the bead, and the ends of the thread are cut approximately ⅛" (3mm) from the knot.

7 Make enough stacks

Repeat layering and stitching until you have created enough pieces to create several rows to cover the ends of your scarf fabric. The finished design features a total of 28 large and 28 small stacked fabric pieces.

8 Attach stacks to the scarf

Alternate sizes and place on the scarf fabric to determine spacing, positioning approximately 1" (3cm) up from each end of the scarf fabric. Stitch in place in each corner with a bead. Knot the thread at the top of the bead and cut the thread ends approximately ⅛" (3mm) from the knots.

9 Watch your spacing

Continue hand-stitching beads in each corner of each piece, spacing rows close together.

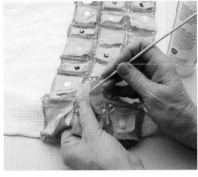

10 Secure the stacks

Squeeze a small puddle of glue onto wax paper. Dip the end of a skewer or toothpick into the glue. Apply a small dab of glue directly underneath the sequin between the dark rose layer and the light green fabric. Lightly squeeze the layers together so the glue gently oozes to catch the layers. (This will keep the pieces from rotating.)

11 Prepare the fringe

Cut the fringe strips into approximately 6" (15cm) lengths. Tie each strip into a knot approximately ⅜" (10mm) from 1 end.

12 Add the fringe

Lay the knotted fringe strips closely along each end of the scarf fabric and machine-stitch or hand-stitch in place.

hints and tips

❀ When ripped, sheer organdy and gauze fabrics create a pretty, tattered edge.

❀ Be sure when ripping fabrics that you leave several inches/centimeters on the side of your first cut in order to tear the fabric.

❀ When applying glue to sheer fabrics, less is best. Do not overapply glue, as it can ooze through and mar the fabric, leaving a stained effect.

T-Shirt Strips

by Heidi Borchers

T-shirts take on an elegant look when cut into strips. Depending on the number of strips you use, you can create a necklace scarf, or add lots of strips for a fuller scarf design. This no-sew design is big on impact and very quick to create.

materials

- 3 large or extra-large T-shirts (without side seams) in complementary colors, patterns and designs (or select white T-shirts and dye to your own color preferences)

- Rotary cutter

- Cutting mat

- Ruler

- Aleene's Fabric Fusion Peel & Stick Sheets

- Nonstick scissors

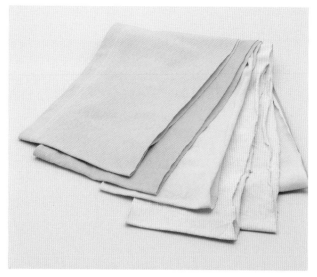

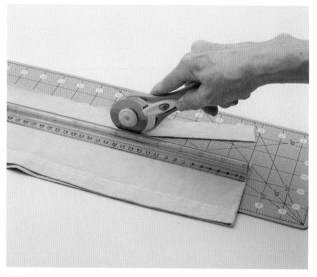

1 Wash and cut your shirts
Wash and dry your shirts. Cut off each T-shirt right below the armpit. Save the top piece to make matching bracelets! If dyeing shirts, the best combination is to dye each shirt 3 different shades of each color. This will give your finished scarf a beautiful ombre effect.

2 Cut into strips
Using a rotary cutter and ruler, mark and cut the T-shirts into 1" (3cm) strips. You will need approximately 20–25 strips for the scarf, or cut more if you want a very full scarf. At this point, your cut pieces should be continuous circles.

hints and tips

♧ Shop your local thrift shop for T-shirts. You can usually find a nice selection of colors, prints and designs at very reasonable prices.

♧ If you shop the fabric store, you can also find plain and printed T-shirt materials in various weights.

♧ If you enjoy customizing, you can purchase T-shirts and dye at your local craft store to create beautiful coloring.

♧ Use a ruler with a finger guard when cutting with a rotary cutter.

♧ It can be helpful to use foamcore and ballpoint pins to pin your strips in place when laying out your finished scarf design.

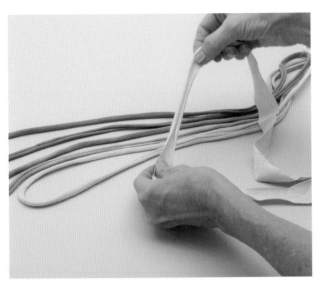

3 Stretch and arrange the strips

Working 6" (15cm) sections at a time, gently pull each fabric strip until the fabric begins to curl along the edges. Once all your pieces are stretched, lay out your pieces to determine the ideal length and placement for your scarf. To create shorter loops for your scarf, cut several stretched pieces to length. To join ends, use scissors to cut 1 piece of peel-and-stick adhesive to ¼" × ⅝" (6mm × 16mm). Remove the paper backing and press the adhesive onto the end of the fabric strip. Remove the secondary paper backing, overlap the ends and press the adhesive to hold the ends together. You should now have a smaller fabric loop.

4 Wrap a cut piece around to finish

When you have the desired layout, select 1 additional stretched fabric piece and cut it to open it into 1 long piece. Use this piece to wrap around and cover the area where you have rejoined the cut edges. Secure the beginning and the end of this strip with small pieces of peel-and-stick adhesive.

Bead Bumps

by Heidi Borchers

This scarf takes on an intriguing texture when you combine organdy and beads. Tucked behind the fabric, glittery beads make a soft statement.

materials

- Organdy fabric—extra soft, lightweight and drapey, in white or a very light color

- Beads—sparkly and glittery, in assorted coordinating colors
  (amount varies depending on preference and size of scarf)

- Rhinestones (amount varies depending on preference and size of scarf)

- Metallic embroidery thread, cut in approximately 8" (20cm) pieces
  (1 piece for each bead)

- E-6000 glue

- Toothpick or wooden skewer

- Scissors

1 Double-check the fabric and beads

For the best effect on this project, you will want to use extra-soft, drapey organdy fabric in very light colors and sparkly or faceted beads.

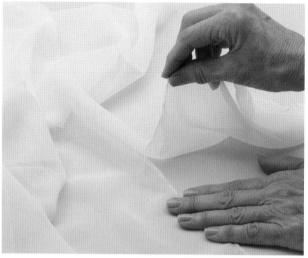

2 Decide the length, width and edges

Determine the desired width and length of the scarf, keeping in mind that the technique of gathering the fabric around the beads will reduce the width and length of the scarf. To create a frayed edge, use scissors to cut a small slit into the fabric. Use both hands to rip the fabric to create frayed edges along the length of the fabric. For frayed ends, cut along the fabric ends and gently pull away the threads to create frayed edges.

hints and tips

✿ Select extra-soft, drapey organdy fabric in very light colors so you can easily see the color, texture and shimmer of the beads.

✿ It's much easier to loop your thread before you insert the bead. That way you can hold the bead with 1 hand, place the looped thread over the bead and then pull the thread ends without the bead popping out.

✿ When inserting the bead into the fabric, be sure to turn it so the holes are on the sides rather than facing out. This will leave the prettiest surface of the bead to show through the fabric.

✿ To preserve the shelf life of your glue, just squeeze out a small dab on a disposable surface and recap the glue right away.

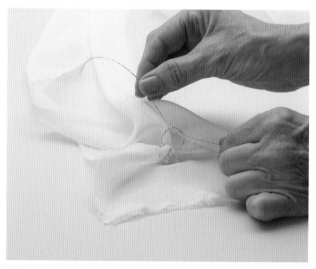

3 Place the first bead

Prepare your thread pieces by looping the ends so you can easily position the thread and pull the ends when it comes time to tie a knot.

Starting at the bottom corner of your scarf fabric, determine the placement of the first bead, approximately 4" to 5" (10cm to 13cm) from the bottom edge and 1 side. Place a bead underneath the fabric and then loop the thread around the bead and fabric and pull the ends to tighten. Loop the ends again and tighten into a knot.

4 Add the remaining beads and tie bows

Repeat step 3 as needed to evenly space and tie all the beads onto the scarf fabric. Tie the knotted thread ends into simple looped bows and secure each bow with a dab of glue. Let the glue dry completely.

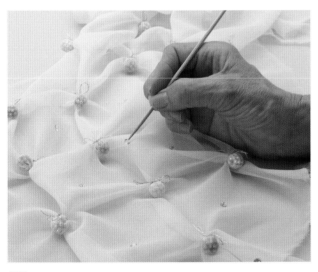

5 Glue the rhinestones onto both sides

To glue rhinestones in place between beads, dip the end of a toothpick or wooden skewer into glue. You need only a small dot of glue on the end of the toothpick. Pick up a rhinestone by pressing the glued toothpick end to the back of the rhinestone. Determine the exact placement of the rhinestone and gently press the edge of the rhinestone onto the fabric while carefully using your finger to guide the glued side of the rhinestone into place on the fabric. Glue rhinestones back-to-back on each side of the fabric. Glue all the rhinestones on 1 side first, then carefully turn over and glue rhinestones on the back side. Because of the sheerness of the fabric, this back-to-back gluing technique will cover up any glue marks on the fabric. Let the glue dry completely.

Hashtags

by Savannah Starr

OMG! This is a fun idea for your BFF. We say #goforit! Hashtags are a cool way to communicate and share the love on this super-fab stenciled scarf.

materials

- Scarf in color of your choice (smooth finish), ironed flat; shown is bamboo rayon
- Fabric paint in color(s) of your choice
- Cosmetic sponge
- Stencil(s)—hashtag, phrases, words
- Scissors or craft knife
- Paper plate (for paint palette)
- Blue painter's tape
- Water and sponge or wet wipes and paper towels (for cleanup)

1 Cut out the stencils

To create your own custom stencil layout, cut out the stencil designs you want to use, leaving as large a border as possible around each stencil.

2 Stencil on the paint

Use blue painter's tape to secure the stencils to the scarf as you work and to join stencils as desired. Place paint on a paper plate. Dip the flat edge of a cosmetic sponge into the paint and dab onto the plate to remove any excess paint. Lightly pounce the sponge up and down over the stencil openings to apply paint to the scarf.

3 Lift stencils and clean before reusing

Lift to reveal the stenciled designs. Clean and dry the stencils thoroughly before reusing. Be certain that the paint is completely dry on the scarf fabric before overlapping and re-aligning stencils over painted areas.

hints and tips

✿ Bamboo rayon is a great fabric for this technique because its very smooth finish is easy to stencil, and the fabric drapes nicely.

✿ A cosmetic wedge sponge is the best applicator for this technique because it holds a lot of paint without oversaturating the fabric.

✿ Dip your sponge into the paint and then dab it about 10 times on the plate to evenly coat the sponge and to remove excess paint. Remember, you can always add more layers of paint!

✿ When dabbing the paint on the stencil, do not press too hard or you will lose the crisp lines of the stencil design.

✿ In order to create crisp stenciled designs, be sure to clean and dry your stencils after each use.

2

summer

Infinity Restyle

by Heidi Borchers

Grab those old knit tops, dresses and thrift store finds and restyle them into an infinity scarf. This no-sew technique is quick and easy for all creative skill levels.

materials

- Knit top or dress (medium or large)
- Aleene's Fabric Fusion Peel & Stick Tape
- Scissors

1 Work with a medium or large
Select a knit wearable from your own wardrobe or check out the thrift store for pretty prints and colors. Medium and large sizes are best for this technique.

2 Cut off the hem
Cut away the bottom hem above the stitching line.

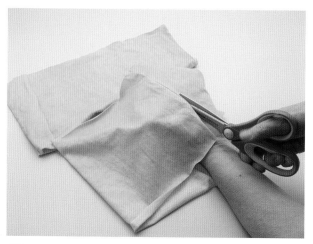

3 Fold up and cut
Fold the bottom edge up to just below the armholes. Using the bottom hemline as a cutting line, cut straight across from armhole to armhole. Save the remaining top piece for another creative project!

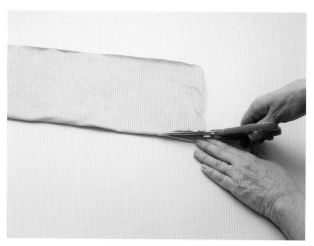

4 Fold in half and cut again
Fold the fabric in half and cut along the fold line to create 2 fabric tubes.

5 Cut off the side seams
Cut along each side of each side seam line, cutting away seam stitching. Repeat on the second piece of fabric. You will now have 2 strips of fabric.

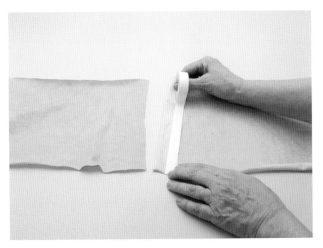

6 Add tape
Apply peel-and-stick tape to the wrong side of 1 end of the fabric.

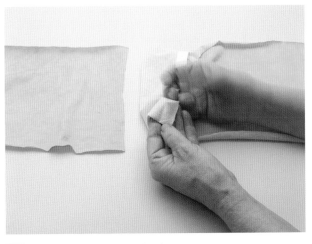

7 Peel away the paper backing
Remove the paper backing from the tape to reveal the adhesive.

8 Join the ends to form a loop
Adhere the 2 pieces of fabric together end to end. Apply tape to the other end and join the ends together. You will now have 1 large infinity loop of fabric.

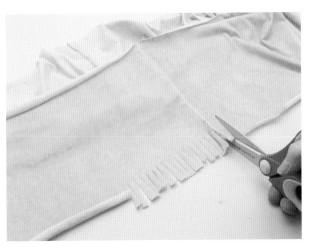

9 Fringe the edges
Fringe the edges of the scarf by cutting in approximately 2" (5cm), spacing your cutting lines ⅜" (10mm) apart (or desired width of fringing).

hints and tips

❁ This technique works great on many different weights of soft fabrics.

❁ For best effect, select fabrics that are similar in color and print on both sides.

Floral Doodles

by Heidi Borchers

Do you love to doodle? Here's a fun way to transform your doodles into wearable works of art. Don't feel artistically inclined? No problem—it's easy to trace a pattern to re-create this floral doodle design.

materials

- Silk scarf (ombre-dyed), ironed flat
- Patterns to trace (see patterns shown later in project)
- White photocopy paper
- .01 and .05 Sakura Pigma Micron pens

1 Go with sheer and a gradation of color

You will need a sheer silk scarf in a light color for this technique. An ombre-dyed scarf also adds some pretty color variation.

2 Transfer patterns to white paper

Transfer the patterns below to white photocopy paper (enlarge to desired size), or sketch out your own designs.

Flower and dragonfly patterns

3 **Trace the main pattern lines onto the silk**
Lay the patterns underneath the scarf in the placement you desire. Using the fine pen tip (.01), trace along the pattern lines. Be sure to use quick strokes, or the pen will easily bleed into the silk fabric. Let the ink dry before the next step.

4 **Add shading**
Use the .05 pen tip to add strokes of shading to the design. For best results, use short, quick strokes.

hints and tips

✿ A silk scarf fabric is recommended for this technique because the pen tips glide easily on the smooth, silky finish.

✿ Be sure that your scarf is ironed flat in order to have a smooth writing surface.

✿ Place the scarf on a smooth, hard writing surface and use your hand to steady the fabric on the pattern while tracing. It's not critical that you follow the pattern lines exactly, but steadying the fabric will help to keep it from shifting while you doodle, trace and draw.

✿ Coloring books are a great source of patterns for this technique.

✿ The silk fabric loves to soak up the ink, so for best design results, keep a light touch and quick stroke with your pen.

Alphabet Flowers

by Tiffany Windsor

It's cool to transform kids' craft foam alphabet letters into blooming florals! Create your own stamps with self-adhesive letters and foamboard.

materials

- Summer-weight scarf (smooth fabric finish)
- Speedball Screen Printing Ink in white
- Craft foam alphabet letters (self-adhesive)—N, C, B, D and O were used to create the flowers shown
- Foamboard
- Large craft foam sheet, 12" × 18" (30cm × 46cm)
- Cosmetic sponges
- Wax paper (small piece for paint palette)
- Craft knife (to cut foamboard)
- Scissors
- Ruler

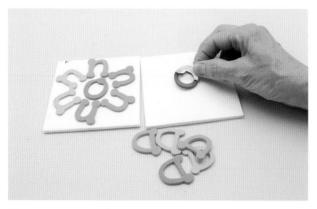

1 Play with arrangement

Measure and cut the foamboard to approximately 4" (10cm) squares to make your letter flower stamps. Arrange the alphabet letters to determine spacing and placement. Remove the paper from the back of an O to expose the adhesive.

2 Place without pressing

Lightly place the O in the center of the foamboard, but do not press it in place yet! Repeat to remove the paper backing from each letter and lightly place them around the flower center. Readjust as needed to center the flower pieces on the foamboard.

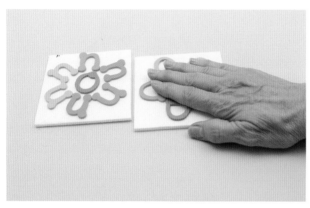

3 Press firmly into place

When all pieces are in the exact desired placement, press down each piece firmly with your fingers.

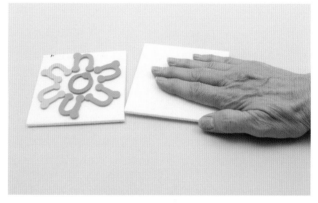

4 Turn over and press again

Turn your stamp over and press firmly on the back of the foamboard.

hints and tips

✤ When working with this technique, be sure to test each stamp on sample fabric first. This will help to determine ink application and stamping pressure.

✤ Move quickly from applying ink to stamping as ink can dry quickly on the stamp.

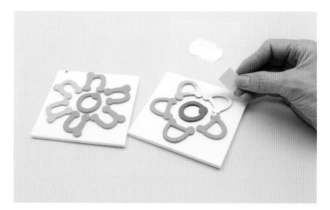

5 Apply ink to the stamp

Pour a quarter-size puddle of ink onto wax paper. Dab a cosmetic sponge into the ink and tap the sponge several times onto wax paper to distribute the ink evenly. Dab the sponge onto the alphabet letters. Let the first coat of ink dry for a few minutes.

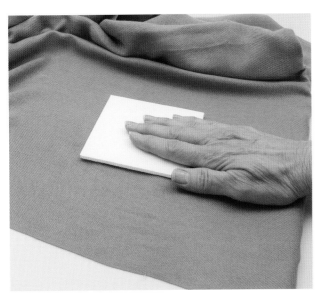

6 Add a second coat, then stamp
Place a craft foam sheet under a single layer of the scarf. Reapply ink onto the stamp and immediately stamp onto the scarf fabric.

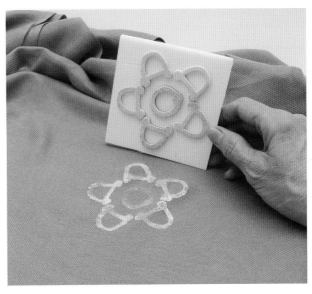

7 Lift and reveal
Lift the stamp to reveal the design.

8 Restamp parts if needed
If any portion of the stamped design does not stamp properly, apply ink to the individual letters, align them over the stamped image and press to transfer the ink. Lift carefully.

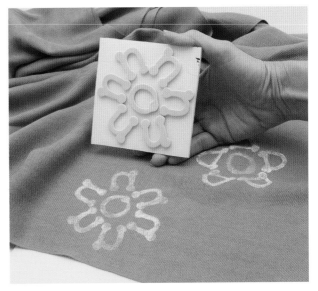

9 Repeat process to add more stamps
Repeat the stamp-making, ink application and fabric-stamping process for each stamp you wish to have, placing each stamped image in a random pattern.

Block-Print Bumblebees

by Heidi Borchers

Linoleum block printing dates back to the early 1900s, but it never goes out of style! Originally carved from linoleum floor covering, block printing supplies are readily available and easy to cut and carve. Simple line drawings turn into works of art with this beautiful technique.

materials

- Medium-weight rayon scarf, 9¼" × 57" (23cm × 145cm)
- Linoleum block, 5" × 7" (13cm × 18cm)
- Large craft foam sheet, 12" × 18" (30cm × 46cm)
- Pattern (for bumblebee shown, see Patterns page in the back of the book)
- Block printing ink and foam tray
- Block cutters with tips of your choice
- Craft knife
- Brayer
- Black permanent marker (medium tip)
- White photocopy paper and a no. 2 pencil
- Blue painter's tape
- Scissors
- Soft brush (optional)

1 Go over the pattern lines
If creating your own design, select your favorite clip art or line art design (or use the bumblebee pattern provided). Use a permanent marker to fatten the lines of the pattern on white photocopy paper.

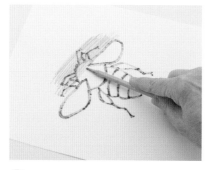

2 Flip over and rub on pencil
Turn the pattern facedown on your work surface and rub a pencil over the entire design.

3 Cut around the pattern
Cut away the excess paper, leaving approximately ½" (13mm) all around the pattern.

4 Tape pencil side down
Tape the pattern to the front of the block, taking care not to tape over any of the pattern lines.

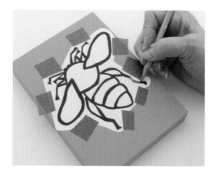

5 Trace the pattern
Trace along all the pattern lines with your pencil, taking time to fill in the thickened lines.

hints and tips

✿ Invest in an additional linoleum block so you can test the cutting tools to find the tool that best suits your pattern design and skill needs.

✿ Block printing kits are a great investment to get started with the block printing technique.

✿ Inks can vary, so if possible, be sure to test the block printing process on a piece of scrap fabric.

✿ If any portion of your design does not print onto the scarf fabric, you can use a fine-line brush to fill it in with ink.

✿ If you are stamping a design off the edge of the fabric, place wax paper on your work surface to catch the extra ink.

6 Lift to reveal transfer
Carefully lift 1 corner to check the pattern. If any trace lines have been missed, press the tape back in place and finish the tracing.

7 Remove the pattern
When all the lines have been fully traced, remove the pattern and set it aside.

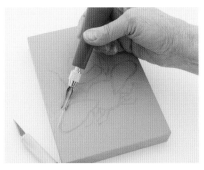

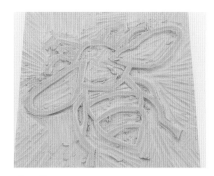

8 Cut away the background
Using a block cutter, begin cutting away the background in short, firm stokes. On some pattern lines it may be helpful to use a craft knife to cut along the pattern lines and then use the scooped cutter.

9 Cut carefully
Continue cutting away the background, working carefully along the outside edge of the pattern so you do not accidently cut into the pattern.

10 Cut away inside areas
Using the same technique, cut away the background from inside the pattern area. Use a soft brush or your hand to gently wipe away all extra pieces of cut block so your block print is free of all scraps.

11 Roll on the ink
Pour a small amount of ink into the tray. Roll a brayer into the ink until the roller is covered with ink, side to side. Roll the brayer on the raised design on the block.

12 Cut away as needed
If any ink was applied to the background, use the cutter to continue to cut away any raised areas of the background.

13 Press onto the scarf
Place craft foam on a flat work surface. Lay the scarf right side up on the craft foam. Reapply the ink and press the block print onto the fabric. Press firmly to transfer the ink to the fabric.

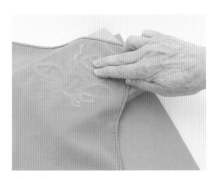

14 Rub to ensure transfer
Keeping the fabric firmly in place, gently lift the block and fabric and flip them onto the craft foam. Use your fingers to continue to rub over the scarf fabric to be certain that all the ink has transferred to the fabric.

15 Lift and let dry
Gently lift the fabric from the block to reveal the printed design. Let the ink dry enough for handling without disturbing the stamped image.

16 Repeat stamping
Repeat the ink application, stamping and rubbing to create additional designs on the scarf, rotating the placement of the designs.

53

Fancy Yarns

by Heidi Borchers

Make it this morning, wear it tonight! Yarn takes on a whole new look with this quick and easy scarf. Cut, braid, knot and go. Knot off fringed ends or add large holed beads for more color and flair.

materials

- Yarn in 7–8 different styles and colors (looped, textured, bumpy, mesh), cut to approximately 8' (2.4m) lengths (Add additional length if a longer scarf is desired.)

    Colors used for the scarf shown (see step 1 photo, from left to right):

    > Lime (bumpy/mesh): 2 strands
    >
    > Teal (mesh): 2 strands
    >
    > Multicolored blues/greens (looped): 2 strands
    >
    > Lavender: 10 strands
    >
    > Light blue: 5 strands
    >
    > Yellow-green: 7 strands
    >
    > Mixed blue (textured): 7 strands

- Assortment of beads with large holes
- Aleene's Original Tacky Glue
- Scissors

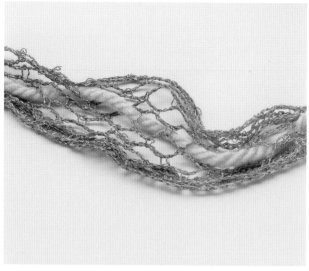

1 Pick a variety of yarns

Select bulky yarns, looped yarns and mesh yarns to create the best texture and volume for this scarf.

2 Weave some strands through mesh yarn

To add additional bulk to your scarf, weave yarn strands through several pieces of mesh yarn. For this scarf 2 light blue strands were threaded through the mesh of 1 lime strand, and single strands of yellow-green and mixed blue were each threaded through strands of teal.

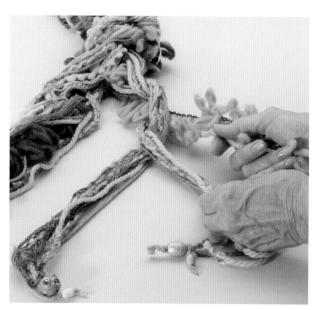

3 Lay out, divide, braid and knot

Lay out the yarn pieces side-by-side on your work table, find the center and tie them together with a piece of yarn. This will help to keep all the yarn pieces in place as you work through the next steps. Working 1 side at a time, divide the yarn pieces into 2 sections and separate. With 1 section, braid for approximately 6" (15cm), join with the unbraided section and tie all strands into a large knot.

4 Repeat techniques for the other side

Repeat the braiding/tying techniques with the other side of the scarf to create coordinating sides. Note that the knots do not have to be aligned exactly.

5 Finish the ends with beads

To finish off the yarn ends, place a dab of tacky glue on the end of each piece of yarn. Press between your fingers to create a pointed end. Add additional glue, press each end into a bead and pull slightly through the other side. When the glue is dry, cut off the excess. Another option is to pull the thread completely through the bead and tie it in a knot. Apply glue to the knot to hold it in place and cut off the excess below the knot. Adjust the bead to fit over the knot.

hints and tips

❧ The thickness of the finished scarf depends on the weight of the yarns selected, so adjust the quantities of the pieces accordingly.

❧ For added bulkiness and texture, create interesting patterning by braiding smaller strands.

❧ Add more color and texture by tying organdy ribbon pieces in random areas.

❧ Be certain to select large-holed beads for the fringed ends. By adding a dab of tacky glue to yarn ends and letting this dry for a few minutes, it will be much easier to thread the yarn ends through the bead holes.

❧ The weight of the beads on the yarn ends helps to add needed weight to this lightweight yarn scarf.

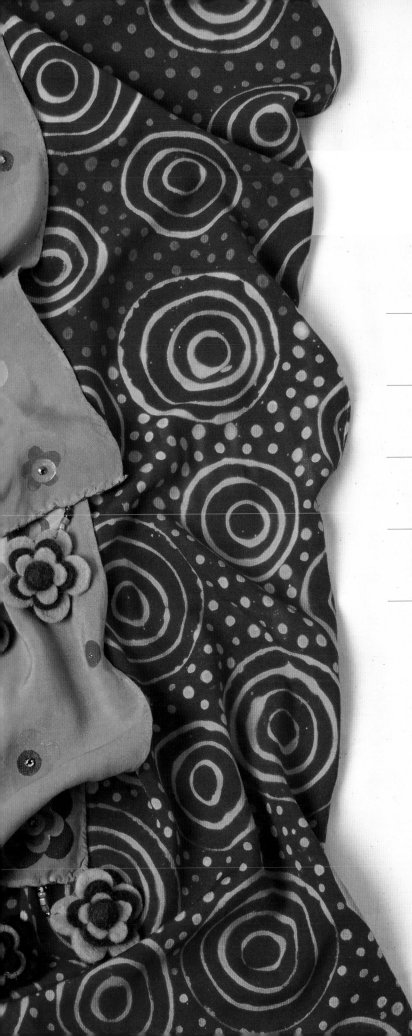

3
autumn

Bleached

by Heidi Borchers and Tiffany Windsor

Create your own patterned scarves with a cool bleaching technique. Natural fibers such as rayon, cotton and linen work well with this technique. Select medium to dark colors for the prettiest contrast in bleaching. Depending on the scarf dye, the patterns turn colors to create one-of-a-kind stamped designs.

materials

- Medium-weight rayon scarf

- Gel bleach pen

- Various sizes of jar lids (design shown features 4 different sizes including canning jar ring, spray paint can lids and paint bottle lid)

- White photocopy paper

- Wax paper

- Wooden skewer (optional)

- Pencil

- Iron

1 Trace circle shapes onto paper

Lay the lids on white paper, leaving space between each lid. Trace around each lid with a pencil. Set the lids aside.

2 Over wax paper add gel bleach

Lay wax paper over the pattern paper. Squeeze a line of gel bleach over the largest pattern line.

3 Dip lid into the circle of bleach

Move the pattern paper and wax paper close to the scarf. Dip the largest lid into the bleach on the wax paper.

4 Press lid onto the fabric

Press the lid onto the scarf, holding it in place for several seconds. The bleaching process will start right away.

5 Lift the lid

Lift the lid carefully to reveal the stamped design. Gently set the lid back on the wax paper until you are ready to use it again.

6 Add more circles

Repeat steps 2–5 to stamp the remaining sizes of lids inside the largest circle design until you stamp the smallest inside circle. Repeat with all the lids to cover the entire scarf with circle designs. After stamping the last circles, let the scarf sit for 15 minutes so the bleach can continue to process. When ready, rinse the scarf in running water to remove the bleach. Hand wash with mild soap. Hang to dry. Iron flat.

hints and tips

✿ This technique does not work on polyester or poly blends.

✿ Depending on the dye used on your scarf, the bleached circles will turn different colors.

✿ Using various shapes, you can create many designs with this technique. The dots in the background of the scarf shown were applied with the blunt end of a wooden skewer.

✿ The lightness of the bleached design will depend on how long the bleach remains on the fabric. If you want each end of the scarf bleached design to match, stamp each end first and continue working your way into the center of the scarf. This will allow the bleach to set the same amount of time as you work to the center of your design.

✿ When working with a bleach pen, follow the label instructions and take care not to get bleach on your skin or clothing.

✿ To control more of the bleaching process, mix a neutralizing solution of 1 part hydrogen peroxide to 10 parts water in a plastic tub before you start your project. This solution will stop the bleaching action when you reach the color you desire. Submerge the scarf in the solution for about 10 minutes, agitating gently. Discard the solution, and handwash the scarf with mild soap.

Stamped & Felted Flowers

by Heidi Borchers

It's fun to use premade embellishments as inspiration for your DIY designs. Readymade wool felted flowers provided the design and color inspiration for this project.

materials

- Medium-weight rayon scarf (solid color), ironed flat

- Readymade felted flowers, 8 each of different sizes, colors of your choice

- Acrylic fabric paint in 2–4 colors of your choice

- Rhinestones

- 40 beads in coordinating colors (holes must be big enough for embroidery thread and needle eye)

- Embroidery thread and needle

- Craft foam

- Foamboard

- Aleene's Original Tacky Glue

- E-6000 glue

- Toothpick (or wooden skewer)

- Cosmetic wedge sponge

- Paper plate (for paint palette)

- Scissors

- Pencil

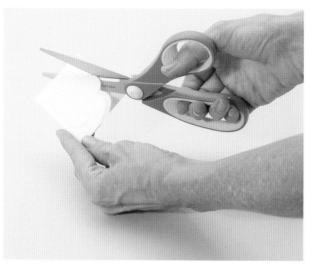

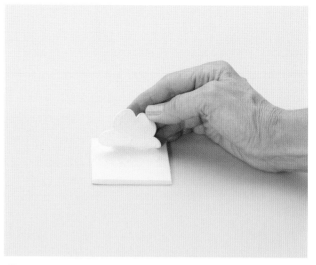

1 Cut flower patterns from foam
With a pencil, trace the 3 sizes of felted flowers (and small circles too, if desired) onto craft foam and cut them out with scissors.

2 Glue foam flowers to foamboard
Glue the craft foam flowers with tacky glue onto pieces of foamboard to create stamps. Let the glue dry.

hints and tips

✿ When dyeing and working with various scarf materials, be sure to test compatibility with dyes. Some fabrics cannot tolerate the hot water needed to set some dyes. We learned that the hard way when the rayon scarf that we dyed for this project took on permanent wrinkles when exposed to hot water in the dyeing process, but we loved the finished result!

✿ When stamping with craft foam, apply 1 thin coat of paint to the stamp, let it dry for a few minutes, then apply a second coat of paint for stamping. This "seasons" the stamp and will extend the working time of the paint.

3 Stamp flower designs onto fabric
Squeeze acrylic paint onto a paper plate. Gently dab the flat edge of a cosmetic sponge into the paint and press it onto the paper plate to spread the paint evenly on the sponge. Then transfer the paint onto a stamp using the sponge, applying a thin layer to the stamp first, letting it dry and then adding a second coat before stamping. Press the stamp onto the fabric and lift it to create the stamped design. Repeat with various colors and stamps, referring to the finished scarf for application ideas. Let dry.

4 Glue on rhinestones

To glue rhinestones in place in the center of your stamped designs, dip the end of a toothpick or skewer into E-6000 glue. You need only a small dot of glue. Pick up a rhinestone by pressing the glued toothpick on the back of it. Determine the exact placement of the rhinestone and gently press the edge of the rhinestone onto the fabric while carefully using your finger to guide the glued side of the rhinestone into place on the fabric. Let the glue dry completely.

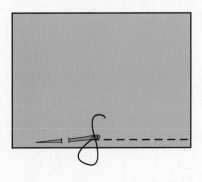

5 Create the fringe

To add flower fringe, thread your needle with embroidery thread. Begin a short running stitch along the bottom edge of the scarf. Add 5 beads to the thread, take the stitch into a felted flower and run the needle back through the beads. Repeat to add more flowers and beads to complete the fringed ends. Tie off the ends of the thread.

How to make a running stitch

✿ To make a running (or straight) stitch, pull your threaded needle up through the wrong side of the fabric and back down through the front with even spacing between your stitches.

Charmed

by Heidi Borchers

Create your own one-of-a-kind, designer-inspired scarf. Make this popular style your very own with charms that have been colored with nail polish. These are so easy, you can make and interchange charm designs to suit your every mood!

materials

- Readymade circle infinity scarf in light-weight T-shirt knit material and color of choice

- Metal charm (flower shown)

- 4 rondelles

- Large metal ring with jump ring added

- Pair of end caps

- Beads: 3 large, 3 medium, 6 small, 1 tiny

- Nail polish in color(s) of your choice

- Needle and coordinating thread

- Eye pins

- Flat-head pins

- Jewelry pliers: flat-head and round-nose

- E-6000 glue

- Wooden skewer

- Scissors

- Optional: lobster claw (to use on charm drop to make it easily interchangeable)

1 **Cut, stitch and gather each end**
Cut across the scarf to create 2 cut ends. Sew a running stitch (see previous project for instructions) along 1 end, gather and tie off. Repeat for the other end.

2 **Color your charm**
Brush nail polish onto your metal charm. Let it dry.

3 **Attach the charm**
Thread the large metal ring onto the scarf. Add 1 rondelle on either side of the metal ring. Slide them into symmetrical positions.

Attach an eye pin to your painted charm and add beads (1 medium, 1 large, 2 small and 1 tiny as shown in the finished project photos). Create an eye hook on the other end of the wire and attach to the jump ring on the large metal ring (see sidebar "How to create and attach an eye hook").

How to create and attach an eye hook

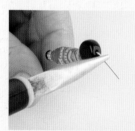

1 **Thread and bend**
Thread beads onto a flat-head pin. Bend the wire 90 degrees at the top of the beads with flatnose pliers.

2 **Trim the wire**
Cut away excess wire, leaving approximately ⅜" (10mm).

3 **Make a loop**
Create a round loop with roundnose pliers.

4 **Attach to another pin**
Attach to the other eye pin or jump ring, closing the loop completely.

4 Add more rondelles and the end caps

If desired, slide 2 additional rondelles onto the scarf in symmetrical positions. Using a wooden skewer, apply E-6000 glue to the stitched ends of the scarf and glue on the end caps.

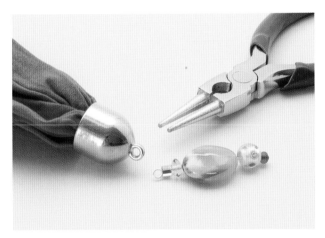

5 Make bead drops for the end caps

Create a bead drop on a flat-head pin (with 1 large, 1 medium and 2 small beads), then form an eye hook (see previous sidebar "How to create and attach an eye hook") and attach it to the end cap. Repeat to create a matching bead drop for the second end cap. Adjust the placement of all rondelles depending on how you wear the scarf.

hints and tips

❧ Another coloring option on metal pieces is alcohol ink. You can apply it by dripping straight from the bottle or using a cosmetic wedge sponge to mix and mottle several colors together. Be sure to apply a brush-on or spray sealer. Test a small sample first to ensure compatibility with alcohol ink. The sealer will keep the color from running.

❧ Create several different variations of charm and bead drops. Add a small lobster claw to easily attach and remove the charms from your scarf.

❧ This is a great project to reuse and recycle other jewelry parts. The center metal ring on this project was recycled from old jewelry. You can create your piece from a decorative rondelle and jump ring. Be creative!

Chain Stitch Embroidery

by Tiffany Windsor

Embroidery is a beautiful technique to add hand-stitched details to any scarf. Not familiar with the encyclopedia of embroidery stitches? No problem! The only embroidery stitch needed for this scarf is the chain stitch. Repeat this stitch to create flowing lines and circles of stitches, or use single stitches to create flower petals.

When stitching on thinner fabrics like rayon, separate the embroidery floss into three strands. For thicker fabrics you can use more strands or switch to yarn to create the chain stitching.

materials

- Medium-weight rayon scarf, finished size 57½" × 9½" (146cm × 24cm)
- Embroidery floss in 11 complementary colors (see step 1 photo for colors used in scarf shown):

    4 shades of brown

    3 shades of green

    2 shades of gold/yellow

    2 shades of orange

- Embroidery needle(s)
- Scissors

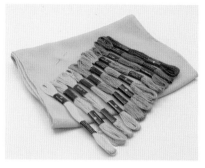

1 **Sort and cut the floss**
Sort the embroidery floss according to color. Cut manageable lengths from the floss for stitching, approximately 1 yard (0.9m).

2 **Thread your needles**
Separate each length of embroidery floss into 2 pieces of 3 strands each. Thread each embroidery needle with 1 color of each floss. Knot an end of each color of floss. Keep the needles in order by sticking them into a scrap piece of fabric.

3 **Set aside the leftover floss**
To keep the remaining 3 strands of floss from tangling, wrap them around 2 fingers and set the circles of thread aside until ready to use.

4 **Start the first chain stitch**
To create the first chain stitch, bring the needle (threaded with your first color) up from the back of the fabric at the bottom of 1 side, letting the knot catch at the back of the fabric.

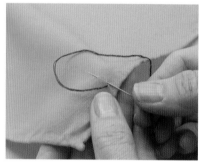

5 **Continue the first stitch**
Reinsert the needle next to the floss and bring it back up approximately ¼" (6mm) from where the needle was first inserted. Keep excess floss looped up and around so the needle will catch it in the next step.

6 **Finish the first stitch**
Gently pull the floss to finish the first chain stitch.

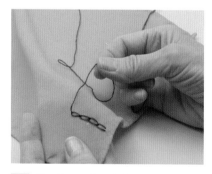

7 **Continue the chain**
Continue to make chain stitches by reinserting the needle next to the floss to create the next chain stitch.

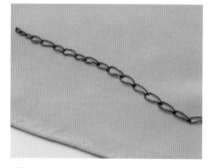

8 **Taper the end**
It's easy to create a meandering line of chain stitches. Note in this design that the final 3 chain stitches are shorter in length in order to create a tapered end to the line of stitches. Knot the thread on the wrong side of the fabric and cut off any excess floss.

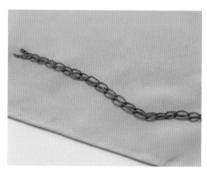

9 **Stitch the second row**
Change to a new floss color. Using the first line of chain stitches as a guide, stitch a second row of chain stitches right next to the first row.

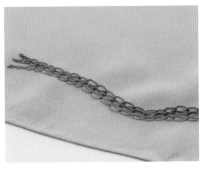

10 Add a third row
Change to a third color of floss and stitch the next row of chain stitches. Note how the last few stitches are curved in a different direction from prior rows.

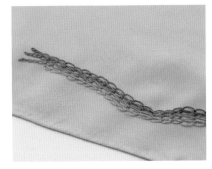

11 Stitch a fourth row
Change to a fourth color of floss and stitch the next row. Note the subtle change in color, which gives an effect of shading.

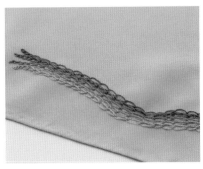

12 Add a fifth row
Change to a fifth color of floss and stitch the next row.

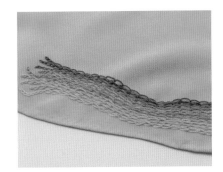

13 Stitch the final rows
Continue to stitch until rows of all colors of the floss have been added.

14 Repeat all
Repeat stitching to create new rows. Note how the flow of lines changes from 1 section to another.

15 Add swirls and petals
Swirls are created by stitching short chain stitches. Start in the center and work outward to create swirls. Petals may be added to the swirls to create flowers. Stitch 1 chain stitch per petal.

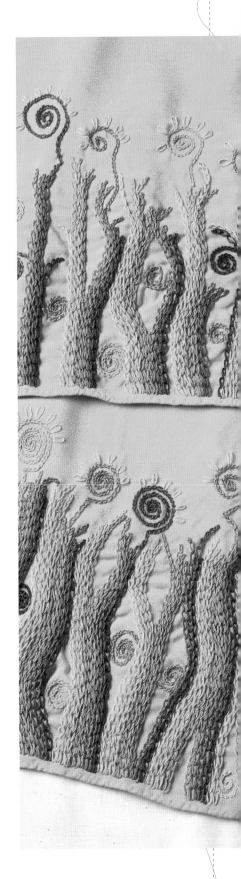

Faux Loomed Woven Yarn

by Tiffany Windsor

Anyone who admires the look of loomed weaving work will love this quick and easy faux loomed design. This is a great technique for crafters who do not knit or crochet but love the look of a handmade loomed scarf.

materials

- Yarns—1 skein each of eyelash fringe, medium bulky and nubby types
- Bridal-style netting with large open weave—approximately 8½" wide × 2 yards (22cm × 1.8m) or adjust for desired finished length
- Large plastic needle
- Scissors

1 **Make sure yarns will work with the chosen netting**
Select yarns that can easily be woven through the netting you have selected as netting patterns can vary.

hints and tips

♣ Bridal netting is available in many different weaves and strengths. Be sure you select a softer netting so your scarf will have a nice drape to it.

♣ An excellent alternative to netting is open-weave mesh yarns.

♣ Slightly fringed and medium bulky yarns are best for this tight weave.

♣ Depending on the size of the weave in your netting, you may need to weave 2 yarn lengths through to fill up the opening. On some rows you can weave in the same up-and-down pattern; on other rows, you may want to alternate the weaving pattern.

♣ With the nubby yarns and the grip of the netting, you should not have to secure the ends of your yarn in place, but if desired, you can knot the yarn pieces at the end of the netting.

♣ Work on a flat, hard work surface and check repeatedly while weaving yarn to make adjustments so the netting remains flat.

2 Thread yarn through the netting

Working directly from the skein, thread the eyelash yarn onto your plastic needle. Weave the tip of the needle up and down along the edge of the netting, pulling gently as you work the length. By following the weave of the netting, you can create straight lines of woven yarns. If your yarns are thinner, weave 2 strands into each row. Pull enough yarn through each row to create fringe on both ends of the scarf. Cut the yarn with scissors. Continue to vary each woven row depending on the finished pattern desired.

3 Trim the fringe

Cut the ends of the yarn straight across to create an even fringe.

4

winter

Pom-Poms & Fleece

by Heidi Borchers

Perfect for those chilly winter days, this no-sew scarf is quick to make. Just mark, snip and wear! Pom-poms add a fun accent on the fleece fringe.

materials

- Fleece fabric, cut to approximately 78" × 12" (198cm × 30cm)
- Yarn, approximately 1 skein (390 yds [357m])
- Pom-pom maker
- Aleene's OK To Wash-It (glue)
- Chalk
- Ruler
- Scissors

1 Mark the short edge
Using chalk and a ruler as a guide, mark the short edge of the fleece every ½" (13mm). Repeat for the other end of the scarf.

2 Make more marks
Measure up 8½" (22cm) from the short edge and mark a horizontal line across. Next, mark the fleece every ½" (13mm). Repeat for the other end.

3 Cut for fringe
Using the marks as a guide, cut ½" (13mm) strips to create 8½" (22cm) fringe on both ends of the fleece.

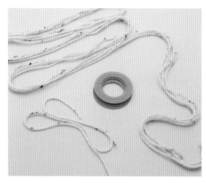

4 Prep for large pom-poms
To create larger pom-poms, cut four 8-yard (7.3m) pieces of yarn and one 12" (30cm) piece of yarn in preparation for making each pom-pom.

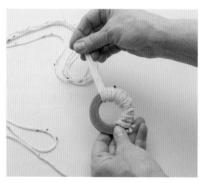

5 Begin the pom-pom
Following your pom-pom maker's instructions, begin wrapping 4 strands of yarn around the maker.

6 Finish wrapping
When finished wrapping, you will have a puffy donut shape of wrapped yarn.

7 Snip the yarn
Following the center groove in the pom-pom maker, snip through the yarn.

8 Tie through the center
Use the 12" (30cm) length of yarn to tie through the center groove. Double knot to hold it securely.

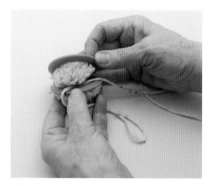

9 Reveal the finished pom-pom
Lift open the maker to reveal the created pom-pom.

10 Trim for roundness

Use scissors to snip the yarn to create a smooth, round pom-pom.

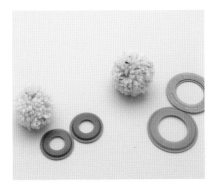

11 Make different sizes

Different sizes of pom-poms can be created with different-size pom-pom makers. The finished sizes of the pom-poms featured on this project are 1¾" (4cm) and 2¼" (6cm).

12 Apply glue

To glue the pom-poms to the end of the fringe, push the yarn aside to find the center of the pom-pom. Apply a dollop of glue to the center.

13 Insert the fleece end into the pom-pom

Insert the end of the fleece fringe into the glue in the center of the pom-pom.

14 Pinch to hold

Pinch with your fingers until the glue begins to hold.

15 Vary pom-pom placement

To glue a pom-pom to the middle of the fringe on some pieces, determine the placement of the pom-pom and cut the fringe at the mark you make.

16 Glue fringe to both sides of pom-pom

Repeat the gluing process to glue fringe to the top and bottom of the pom-pom.

hints and tips

✿ For best results, select high-quality soft fleece for the scarf fabric.

✿ Fleece fabric is a great fabric to use for this type of project because it does not fray when cut.

✿ Pom-pom makers come in many different shapes and sizes and work in many different ways to create pom-poms. The pom-pom maker in this demonstration created the fullest and densest pom-poms.

Finger Crochet

by Tiffany Windsor

Toss your crochet hook aside! This fluffy scarf is made with rows of single crochet, but you don't need a hook. Using your hands and fingers, you can quickly crochet a neck warmer or a full-length scarf.

Fluffy, chenille-type yarns work great for this project. You can select skeins of the same color or use complementary or contrasting colors. For ease of use when crocheting, it is helpful to roll your yarn into balls.

materials

- Fluffy yarn: 2–3 skeins, depending on the yardage of each skein; scarf shown was created with 2 skeins of Patons Bohemian yarn (68 yards [62m] each) in Peaceful Plum (#11310)

- Large 1½" (4cm) decorative button (LaMode button shown)

- Needle and thread

- Embroidery floss for button (or needle and thread)

- Scissors

1 Start a chain stitch

To create the first row of chain stitches, hold the ends of 2 strands of yarn in your hand and wrap around your other hand, crossing over the front.

2 Prepare to pull

To prepare for pulling through the yarn, reach through the 2 strands on the back of your hand.

3 Grab and pull

Grab 2 strands and gently pull through the yarn on the back of your hand.

4 Finish the first chain loop

Gently pull to create the first chain. Be certain to leave a large loop so it is easier to pull through the yarn in the next steps.

5 Repeat

Repeat the process by gently pulling the 2 strands of yarn through the loop.

6 Make a loop of similar size

Pull enough yarn through to create a loop of similar size to the first chain loop.

hints and tips

✿ Select fluffy, full-bodied yarns for this technique.

✿ Just like when you are crocheting with a hook, the key in this technique is to keep your loops large and loose. If you pull too tightly, it will be difficult to pull the 2 strands of yarn through the loops.

7 Continue adding stitches

Continue to create the next chain stitch, again matching size to the first loops. Continue to create chain stitches until you reach the desired width of the scarf (the finished example is 9 chains wide).

8 Start a single crochet stitch

To prepare for your first single crochet stitch, hold the final chain stitch in 1 hand and hold open the last chain stitch with your other hand.

9 **Reach through, pull and loop**
Reach through the chain stitch and pull and loop 2 strands of yarn on your hand. (You will now have 4 strands of yarn on your hand.)

10 **Reach through both loops**
Reach your fingers through the 2 loops in preparation for grabbing the 2 strands of yarn. Be sure to keep the loop large so you have enough room to pull through.

11 **Pull 2 strands**
Pull the 2 strands of yarn through to create the first single crochet.

12 **Continue single crochets**
Reach through each chain stitch, looping and then pulling the yarn through, to complete a row of 8 single crochets. When you reach the last stitch in the row, turn the piece over and continue to build rows of single crochet, turning at the end of each row.

13 **Finish the ends**
The neck warmer measures about 9" × 34" (23cm × 86cm). When you reach the end, cut off the yarn, leaving 6" (15cm) tails. Pull the tails through the loop and pull snuggly to knot. Weave the yarn ends back into the scarf. Use a needle and thread to stitch the ends in place so they do not pull out.

14 **Fold over the right**
To determine the placement of the button, lay the scarf flat on your work surface and fold over the right end at a slight angle.

15 **Fold over the left**
Loosely fold over the opposite end, leaving enough space in the center to accommodate your neck when wearing the scarf. Cut a 12" (30cm) length of embroidery floss and thread it through the button shank.

16 **Place and attach the button**
Determine the exact placement of the button and tie it in place on the bottom layer. Loop the top yarn over the button to hold the scarf in place.

Embossed Velvet Hoodie

by Savannah Starr

An exercise hoodie takes on a new look when combined with velvet to create a stylish scarf perfect for a winter wonderland walk. The special technique of embossing velvet makes this scarf a one-of-a-kind gift.

materials

- White hoodie sweatshirt with drawstring tie
- Velvet: 2 pieces, 9½" × 48" (24cm × 122cm)
- Rubber stamp (must be bold rubber stamp design mounted on wood block)
- Needle or sewing machine and thread (to match hoodie and velvet)
- Straight pins
- Aleene's Fabric Fusion Peel & Stick Sheets
- Spray bottle with water
- Nonstick scissors
- Iron (preferably without steam holes) and firm, nonslip ironing surface

hints and tips

♧ It is best to test the velvet embossing technique on a sample piece first. It is important to get the correct setting on your iron while not scorching the velvet. Test, test, test!

♧ This project can be created in any combination of hoodie and velvet colors.

♧ When selecting a stamped design for the velvet, be sure to select stamps with a broad surface. This embossing technique does not work well with finely detailed stamp designs.

♧ If you do not sew, this entire project can be assembled and finished off with the peel-and-stick adhesive sheets.

♧ For a fun finishing touch, glue strips of fun fur around the edge of the hoodie with peel-and-stick adhesive.

1 Cut off the hoodie
Carefully cut off the hoodie from the sweatshirt above the stitching at the neckline. Cut away the remaining zipper but leave the drawstring tie in place and uncut.

2 Stitch and emboss the velvet
Pin and stitch the velvet pieces right sides together along the 9½" (24cm) edge. To emboss, place the stamp faceup on your ironing surface. Spritz the wrong side of the velvet with water and place the fuzzy side down on the stamp. With your iron set to medium low, set the iron directly on the velvet and hold for about 5 seconds, then lift the iron straight up. Carefully lift 1 edge of the velvet to see if the pattern has embossed cleanly. If it did not, carefully place the velvet back on the rubber stamp, spritz lightly again with water on the wrong side, and iron again for about 7 seconds. If the design is clearly embossed, lift the velvet from the stamp. Repeat this technique to make a repeat or random pattern on the velvet.

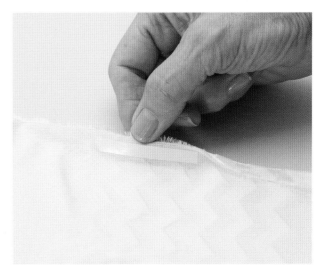

3 Stitch the velvet to the hoodie

Align the stitched seam of the velvet with the center back of the hoodie and pin into place, right sides together. Stitch the velvet to the hoodie. To hold stitched edges flat, cut ¼" × 2" (6mm × 5cm) pieces of peel-and-stick adhesive and apply to the wrong sides of the seam fabric. Remove the paper backing and press the fabric flat to hold the stitched edges flat. Turn the edges and hand-stitch any exposed fabric edges on the hoodie.

4 Finish the velvet edges

To hem the remaining edges of the velvet, cut more ¼" (6mm) strips of peel-and-stick adhesive and apply them to the wrong edge of the velvet. Working in small sections at a time, remove the paper backing, fold over the edges and press for the adhesive to hold.

Mad About Plaid

by Heidi Borchers

Men's flannel plaid shirts can be mixed and matched to create light winter-weight scarves. Add a useful touch by incorporating the shirt pockets into your design.

materials

- Men's (or women's) flannel shirts, extra-large
- Sewing machine and matching thread
- Scissors
- Iron

1 Choose shirts similar in weight

Select flannel shirts that are similar in weight. It's a great look when you mix and match designs in the same colors.

2 Cut and position the pieces

Determine the desired finished size (our finished example is 9¾" × 67" [25cm × 170cm]) and cut your shirts into strips, squares and rectangles that when put together will fit these dimensions. Remember that you can also incorporate shirt plackets, buttons or pockets. Lay out all of your pieces neatly on your work surface.

3 Stitch them together

Working 1 row at a time, lay the pieces right sides together and stitch them together with a ½" (13mm) seam allowance.

hints and tips

❧ Thrift stores have lots of men's flannel shirts. Select the largest shirts you can find (one of ours was 4X) so you can get the most fabric cuts.

❧ Depending on the finished look you want, you can stitch pieces together with hidden or exposed seams.

❧ For an added color punch, you can line this scarf in a bright color or add patches of fun designs and colors.

4 Trim the seam allowances
Cut away the seam allowances to ¼" (6mm).

5 Topstitch
When all the pieces are sewn together and the seam allowances are cut, topstitch ⅛" (3mm) from the seam lines.

6 Add extra pieces for interest
To add decorative detail, cut contrasting patterns and stitch them onto the scarf using zigzag stitches.

7 Hem the edges
Hem each edge by turning it over ⅛" (3mm) and ironing to hold the fold. Roll over ⅛" (3mm) again and stitch to hem all 4 edges.

5

couture

Felted Fantasy Scarflet

by Sara Smelt, guest artist

Felt, the oldest textile known to man, is created by adding soap, water and agitation to loose bundles of wool fiber referred to as "roving." By hand-working the wool and adding silk and other fibers, you can create an autumn-inspired wet-felted scarflet.

materials

- Merino wool roving in Eggplant, Olive, Cinnabar and Burnt Orange (0.8–1 oz [24–30ml] of each color)
- Merino wool roving in Gold (0.1 oz [30ml])
- Small amount of complementary-colored silk tops, mohair locks and silk gauze
- Bubble wrap, 64" × 24" (163cm × 61cm)
- Nylon netting, 64" × 24" (163cm × 61cm) (sheer curtain material is ideal; check your local thrift store)
- Embroidery floss (or sewing machine and thread) in leaf green, purple
- Needle and thread (for button)
- Button or brooch
- 2 plastic tubs

- 3 ties (use knee-high nylon stockings or strips of spandex)
- Foam pool noodle
- Pens or wooden skewers
- Bath towel
- Dish soap
- Spray bottle
- White vinegar
- Scissors
- Iron and ironing board
- 6' (1.8m) table (or a clean floor)
- Ruler

hints and tips

♣ Merino wool roving is available in many beautiful dyed colors, so you can create beautiful designer-inspired color combinations.

♣ Wool shrinks as it felts. To create a scarflet approximately 33" (84cm) in length, lay out a 50" (127cm) rectangle. This allows for 34-percent shrinkage. If you would prefer a longer or shorter scarf, adjust the measurements accordingly.

1 Split the wool in half
Lay the bubble wrap (bubbles up) on the table. Split each color of merino wool in half.

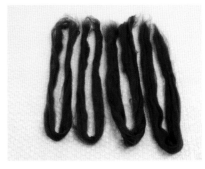

2 Split in half again
Split each color of merino wool in half again to create 4 lengths. Put one-fourth of each color aside.

3 Pick up the roving
Hold a length of Eggplant and Olive roving in 1 hand and hold the very ends of the roving between the tips of your fingers and the heel of the palm of your other hand.

4 Pull out a tuft
Gently pull out a fine tuft of wool. If the tuft comes out too thick, hold it at each end and divide it again.

5 Lay out a column
Lay a tuft of the Olive and Eggplant roving horizontally 1" (3cm) from the top edge and approximately 10" (25cm) from the right side edge of the bubble wrap. Create a 14" (36cm) column of slightly overlapping horizontal pieces of wool.

6 Lay out more overlapping columns
Continue laying the Olive and Eggplant roving in slightly overlapping columns to create a 50" × 14" (127cm × 36cm) rectangle.

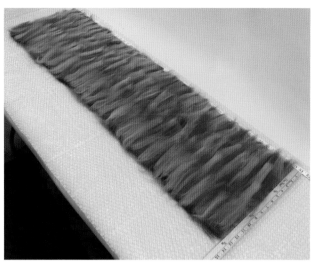

7 **Lay rows across the columns**
Create a second layer by laying the Cinnabar and Burnt Orange wool in rows across the rectangle. Lay the fibers at a 90-degree angle (a quarter turn) to the first layer.

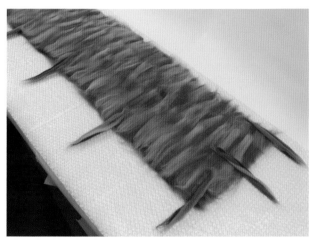

8 **Form the fronds**
Make the fronds by dividing the roving that was set aside (one-fourth of each color) into 4 lengths (1/16 of the original rope of wool). Combine 3 colors (3 × 1/16) of wool and make 17 fronds 7" to 8" (18cm to 20cm) in length.

Evenly arrange 5 fronds along the lower long edge of the scarf and 2 fronds on the right side edge. Overlap the edges of the scarf by 3" (8cm).

9 **Make and add the leaves**
Shape 8 leaves (4" [10cm] long) with a small amount of roving. Lay these on top of the fronds, leaving 1" (3cm) of the stem visible. Add 2 fronds and a length of mohair between each leaf on the lower edge of the scarf. Add 1 frond and 1 length of mohair between each leaf on the side edge. If you do not have mohair locks, add another frond. Make the fronds assorted lengths.

10 **Add a third layer**
Create the third layer by holding a piece each of Egg-plant, Olive, Cinnabar and Burnt Orange roving in your hand and laying the fibers in the same direction as the first layer. If desired, add a small amount of Gold wool to the third layer.

11 Add accents
Decorate the surface with pieces of silk tops (for shine) and leaf-shaped pieces of silk gauze (for texture). Add very fine pieces of Gold wool on top to help them felt into the scarf.

12 Cover with nylon netting
Carefully begin to roll out the nylon netting over the scarf, taking care not to disturb the wool or gauze pieces. Cover the entire scarf with nylon netting.

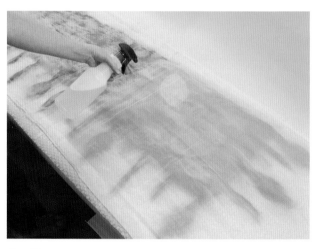

13 Spray the netting
Spray the netting with hot soapy water (a few drops of dish soap in a spray bottle of hot water).

14 Press down
Press straight down on the roving to begin to compact it and distribute the soapy water. Continue pressing to distribute the soapy water, spraying any remaining dry areas.

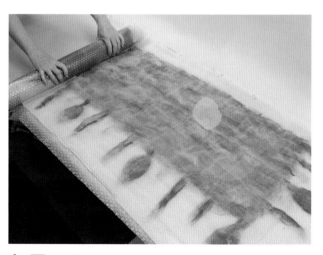

15 Roll it up
Roll the scarf bundle (including the bubble wrap) around the foam noodle.

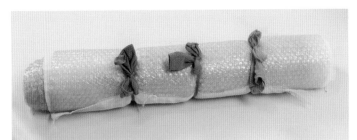

16 Tie the bundle
Secure with 3 ties.

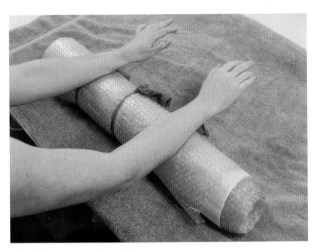

17 Roll back and forth
Roll the bundle back and forth from your fingers to your elbows for 3 minutes.

18 Unroll and smooth out
Unroll the bundle and gently remove the nylon netting. Take care to brush down any fibers that have attached to the nylon netting. Gently stretch out any wrinkles in the scarf.

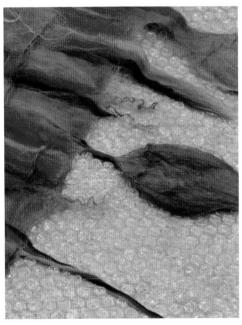

19 Roll the fronds and continue rolling the bundle
Roll each of the fronds back and forth to create cords. Start gently and gradually increase your pressure. Cover the scarf with the nylon netting and roll the bundle onto the foam noodle starting from the opposite end. Repeat the rolling process an additional 3 times, for 5 minutes each time. Unroll and check the scarf after each 5 minutes. Roll the fronds each time. Roll up the bundle from the other end each time. Unroll the scarf and turn it over. Do 2 additional 5-minute rolls, unrolling and checking after each set.

20 Turn the scarf over and test

Turn it over to reveal the back side of the scarf. Apply the pinch test: Pinch a small area of the scarf between your thumb and first finger. If the scarf lifts up in 1 piece, it is ready for the final steps. If individual fibers lift up, continue to roll in 5-minute batches.

21 Submerge and squeeze

Fill 1 tub with cold water and a second tub with hot water that is comfortable for your hands. Squeeze the scarf in the hot water for 30 seconds. Plunge it into the cold water and squeeze it for 30 seconds. Repeat the hot water/cold water steps again. The felt will become thicker during this stage.

22 Work out any lumps

Lay out the scarf. Gently pry apart any areas that may have become stuck together. The edges of the scarf are particularly prone to rolling over and sticking. Take time to smooth them to prevent lumpy edges.

23 Throw scarf and repeat water process

Lightly throw the scarf against the table 10 times. Repeat the hot water/cold water process (step 21). Lay out the scarf and shape the edges. Throw the scarf 20 times. Continue the hot water/cold water and throw steps until you are happy with the size and texture of the scarf (usually 1–3 rounds total).

24 Rinse and soak in vinegar water
Rinse out the soap and soak the scarf in a tub of cool water containing ⅛ cup (30ml) of white vinegar for 10 minutes.

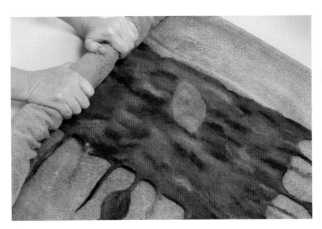

25 Rinse and roll
Rinse the scarf and roll it up in a towel to remove excess water.

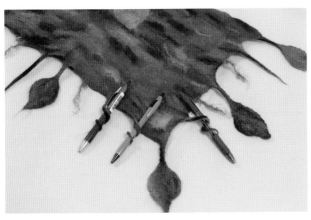

26 Shape the scarf and spiral the fronds
Shape the scarf, iron it to smooth the felt and lay it flat to dry. Wrap the fronds around pens or wooden skewers to create spirals (felt maintains the shape in which it dries).

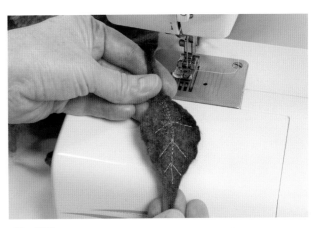

27 Add veins to leaves
Machine stitch or embroider veins onto the leaves.

28 Add a button
Sew a button onto your scarf. (Or use a brooch to secure the scarf.)

29 Cut a buttonhole
Determine the buttonhole location. Cut open it with scissors.

Full of Hearts

by Tiffany Windsor

Inspired by a trip to the local thrift store where the women's T-shirts are sorted by colors, this collection of layered hearts shares complementary color combinations. Arranged on black, these hearts pop with pretty colors on this joyful scarf that's perfect for the heart lover!

materials

- Black rayon fringed scarf, finished measurements 13¾" × 60" (35cm × 152cm)

- T-shirts in complementary colors: rose (3 shades), tangerine (3 shades), salmon (3 shades)

- Heart patterns, transferred and cut out of cardstock or manila folders (for the hearts shown, see Patterns page in the back of the book)

- Black thread

- Ruler

- Scissors

- Sewing machine

hints and tips

❧ Take your time with the initial layout of this scarf. Even though you lay everything out and then take it off, this will be very helpful when it comes time to start stitching the pieces.

❧ When stitching stretchy T-shirt material to the rayon scarf, you will need to adjust (raise and lower) the presser foot on your sewing machine several times as you stitch around the curved sections of the hearts. This will help ease the fabric to keep it flat.

1 Cut the fabrics flat
Cut the sleeves from the T-shirts, and also the neck band and hem. Cut along the shoulder and side seams to create flat fabric pieces.

2 Cut out heart patterns
Use the patterns to cut out 100 each small, medium and large hearts from the fabrics. Use the sleeves to cut the smaller hearts.

3 Stack the hearts
Stack large, medium and small hearts of the same color range.

4 Lay out the first row
It is helpful to first lay out all the stacked hearts on the scarf to determine placement and measurements. Starting with the first row, align 5 stacked hearts along the edge, matching the tips of the large heart with the ends of the fringe. Keep in mind that you do not need to be exact because the next several steps are for layout purposes only.

5 Add the second row
Place 4 stacked hearts for the second row, alternating with the first row.

6 Add the third row
Place 5 stacked hearts for the third row, alternating with the second row.

7 Add the fourth row
Place 4 stacked hearts for the fourth row, alternating with the third row.

8 Add the fifth row
Place 5 stacked hearts for the fifth row, alternating with the fourth row.

110

9 Add the sixth row
Place 4 stacked hearts for the sixth row, alternating with the fifth row.

10 Add the seventh row
Place 5 stacked hearts for the seventh row, alternating with the sixth row. Use a ruler to check placement measurements.

11 Begin the center section
For the center portion of the scarf, begin laying out individual hearts in each color collection.

12 Overlap randomly
Space each collection of small, medium and large hearts overlapping in different directions.

13 Cover the entire area
If needed, cut additional hearts to cover the entire center section of the scarf. Once the layout is complete, carefully remove the hearts to your side table to prepare for sewing them in place.

14 Start topstitching
The first 5 rows are topstitched in place with straight lines at the top of the large hearts and the top of the small hearts.

15 Continue stitching
For the sixth row, topstitch all the way around the small heart and around the top of the medium and large hearts. For the seventh (last) row, topstitch all the way around the small and medium hearts. This bright scarf has a casual and playful feel, so don't worry if your stitching is not completely straight.

16 Tack the large hearts
Machine tack the tops of the large hearts to the scarf in the seventh (last) row.

17 Topstitch the center hearts
Topstitch all the way around each individual heart in the center area.

Looped Fabric Strips

by Heidi Borchers

Simple strips of fabric can be layered to create a striking scarf design. Upcycle thrift store dresses or purchase fabric by the yard to mix and match designs for a fabulously loopy look!

materials

- Thrift store dresses (rayon fabric)
- Matching thread
- Plain newsprint or packing paper
- Large marking pen (for looping fabric)
- Rotary cutter and mat
- Ruler
- Straight pins
- Scissors
- Sewing machine

1 Select fabrics carefully

For ease of layout and stitching, select fabrics that are the same thickness. Long rayon dresses from a thrift store are a great choice. Select patterns and colors that complement each other.

2 Start cutting

Cut along 1 side seam of a dress. Cut away the top portion of the dress so you are left with 1 large piece of fabric. Fold the fabric back and forth to create 4 layers. Place the folded fabric on a cutting mat and align the bottom edges of the hem. Use a rotary cutter to cut off the hem. Set aside. Use a rotary cutter to cut 1" (3cm) strips from the bottom of the dress.

3 Cut more strips

Cut 1" (3cm) strips from all the fabrics. The strips will need to be joined together to create the lengths needed for this project. Join the strips by machine stitching with a ¼" (6mm) seam. Cut to create strips that are approximately 13' (4m) in length. This will allow for fringe on both ends and 36 rows of 3" (8cm) loops. The scarf shown was created with about 60 strips.

4 Prepare the paper

The background paper is designed to act as a stitching base and then will be torn away when all sewing is completed. Cut several strips of paper approximately 8" (20cm) wide. Overlap the ends and machine stitch them together to create the needed length. Cut the paper to approximately 66" (168cm) long × 8" (20cm) wide. (If you wish, you can tape the pieces of paper together, but be sure the tape you use will not gum up the machine needle in the next steps.)

5 Lay out the strips on the paper

Begin laying out the fabric strips on the background paper. Approximately 10 rows will fit across the paper. To create the fringe, leave approximately 8"–9" (20–23cm) overhanging at the end of the paper.

6 Layer and pin

Continue to layer the strips until you have 6 layers. Approximately 1" (3cm) in from the end of the paper, pin each row (6 pieces) in place on the background paper.

7 Check the pins

Check the paper side to be sure the pins are securely in place and are lined up evenly.

114

8 **Stitch the first line**
With pins holding the rows in place, machine stitch the first stitching line using the pins as a guide. This will secure the strips to the paper.

9 **Insert the pen**
To create the loops, working small (3" [8cm]) sections at a time, insert the pen underneath 3 layers of fabric strips. This will leave 3 strips flat on the paper and 3 strips with a loop.

10 **Stitch the second line**
Keeping the pen snug against the first stitch line, and fabric strips looped over the pen, begin the second stitch line. Keep checking to be sure the pen fits snugly against the first stitch line. This will help you keep the second stitch line straight while holding up the loops.

11 **Stitch for more loops**
Keep moving the pen down and looping the fabric strips as you stitch in order to stitch the loops in place on the paper.

12 **Finish stitching and remove the paper**
Continue the same stitching technique to complete all stitched loop rows. Turn the stitched piece over and tear away the paper backing.

13 **Make the fringe**
Measure and cut the strips to the desired length on each end for the fringe.

hints and tips

❧ When selecting dresses for this scarf, choose the largest sizes you can find. This scarf was created with 3 XL rayon dresses.

❧ Even with the guide of the marking pen to hold the loops, it can be challenging to create exact loop sizes consistently with this technique. So don't worry about stitching each row with the exact same loop height, as this will give added interest to your design.

❧ If you prefer to use a fabric base for the scarf, replace the paper with a piece of backing fabric cut to size.

❧ If using paper backing, replace your sewing machine needle after this project as stitching on paper will dull your needle.

Felt & Organdy Blooms

by Heidi Borchers

Felt and organdy circles are transformed into a burst of blooms on this high-style scarf. Premium felt is soft and slightly stretchable, which gives these flowers more dimension.

materials

- Lightweight gauze scarf (slightly stretchy, tapered at the ends); see "hints and tips" sidebar for recommended size

- 44" (112cm) wide premium felt in coral, buttercup yellow and ivory, ¾ yard (0.7m) of each color

- 44" (112cm) wide organdy in white or ivory, 1¼ yards (1.1m)

- Beads

- Circle patterns, transferred and cut out of cardstock or manila folders (for the circles shown, see Patterns page in the back of the book)

- Aleene's Fabric Fusion Peel & Stick Tape

- Needle and thread

- Scissors

1 Cut out all the circles

Hold each pattern in place on the felt and cut out small, medium and large circles from each color of felt. Cut small and large organdy circles and ½" circles of felt (for the back). The finished design features approximately 130 layered circle flowers.

2 Stretch the large circles

To give body and dimension to the flowers, hold the large felt circles in your hands and gently pull to stretch them along the edges.

3 Flute the large circles

Press your thumb into the center of the stretched circle and pull around the outside edge to create a slightly fluted effect.

4 Layer each flower

To layer a flower, begin with a largest felt circle, then layer with a large organdy, medium felt, small organdy and small felt.

hints and tips

♣ The base scarf on this project measures 70" (178cm) long and tapers from 11" (28cm) wide at the neckline to 2½" (6cm) wide at the ends, giving the finished design a lot of bulk at the neck and shoulders and tapering down to a few flowers at the tips.

♣ For the base scarf, be sure to select a soft, lightweight, drapey fabric, but make sure it is strong enough to hold the weight of the felt.

♣ Want to start with a smaller project? Create a few of these layered circle flowers for a lapel pin, headband or barrette.

5 Vary the combinations

Vary your felt circles to create different color combinations for your flowers.

6 Start attaching flowers

Use a needle and thread to attach your flowers to the scarf. Knot the end of the thread. Place the stacked piece on the right side of the scarf, and bring the needle up from wrong side of the scarf and through the center of the flower.

7 Add a bead

Add a bead to the needle and press the needle back through the center of the flower.

8 Pull to fit snugly

Check to be sure the bead fits snugly at the center of the flower and that the thread is pulled tightly.

9 **Add a small circle to back**
Stitch the needle and thread through a ½" (13mm) circle of felt to the back of the scarf with several single stitches. Knot the thread and cut away the excess.

10 **Stitch flowers close together**
To give added dimension to the flowers on your scarf, stitch them in place close enough together that the edges of each flower are supported and raised by the next flower. Repeat to cover the entire scarf with flowers.

11 **Use peel-and-stick tape**
To help keep the petals raised, cut a ¼" (6mm) piece of peel-and-stick tape and attach it to the back edge where the petals meet. Remove the release paper to expose the adhesive.

12 **Adhere the petals to each other**
Pinch the felt together so the adhesive holds firmly.

13 **Add more flowers**
Continue adding flowers until the scarf is completely covered and finished.

Painted Plastic Printing

by Heidi Borchers

Add an artistic touch to fabric with this super-easy technique. By painting on plastic sheets and printing on fabric, you can create beautiful hand-printed designs. Even the beginning painter will find that using simple geometric shapes for the print patterns makes this method easy to do! For best results, select a smooth-finish fabric for printing on your designs. When you first start this technique, it is best to start with small sections at a time as the paint can start to dry quickly on the plastic.

materials

- Silkessence polyester fabric (finished scarf is 39½" × 93" [100cm × 236cm])

- Clear shrink plastic sheet (or other clear rigid plastic), 8½" × 11" (22cm × 28cm)

- Jacquard Textile Colors (2.25oz [67ml] jars): Maroon 109 (2 jars), Violet 110 (2 jars), Turquoise 114 (1 jar)

- Soft-bristle brushes: small round and ½" (13mm) flat

- Wax paper

- Cardboard tube (from gift wrap)

- Transparent tape

- Wet wipes

- Paper towels

- Water

1 Prepare your work surface

Cover your work surface with strips of wax paper. To keep the wax paper from shifting, tape the edges together. To keep the fabric from shifting during the printing process, tape the end of the fabric to the wax paper.

2 Start applying paint to plastic

To manage the large piece of fabric, roll up the excess onto a gift-wrap tube so you can work on small sections of fabric at a time. Place clear plastic on the wax paper along with the textile paint jars. Dip your ½" (13mm) flat brush into Maroon and brush zigzag lines onto the plastic.

3 Add another line

Immediately brush a Violet zigzag line next to the first painted line.

4 Press plastic onto fabric

Lift up the plastic, align it facedown on the edge of the fabric and rub the plastic with your fingers to transfer the painted design.

5 Lift to reveal print

Quickly lift to reveal the printed design.

6 Reapply paint to plastic

If continuing the same design and colors, you don't need to clean the plastic yet. Reapply the paint by brushing it on the plastic in the same pattern.

7 Print again

It is easy to see through the plastic to align the next painted pattern. Rub the plastic with your hands and lift it to reveal the design.

8 Clean the plastic when changing patterns

When you want to switch to a new pattern, clean the plastic with a wet wipe and dry with a paper towel.

9 Paint a different design

Paint the next design (triangles and lines) on the plastic, being careful not to overapply paint. In this technique you want to see the brushstrokes, so a thinner application of paint works well.

10 Press again to transfer

Press the painted design facedown on the fabric and rub the plastic with your fingers. In this step the pattern does not align exactly.

11 Lift and clean the plastic

Lift to reveal the design. Clean the plastic with a wet wipe and dry with a paper towel.

12 Paint squares on the plastic

Paint the next design of multicolor squares on the plastic.

13 Transfer the print

Press the squares design onto the fabric and rub the plastic with your fingers to transfer the square painted designs onto the fabric.

14 Lift and clean the plastic again

Lift the plastic to reveal the printed square designs. Clean the plastic with a wet wipe and dry it with a paper towel.

15 Fill in the gaps

If needed, apply paint directly to the fabric to fill in any gaps in the design. Dip the end of your brush in paint and brush light paint strokes on the fabric. Single strokes create the best effect.

16 Create shading with additional colors

Additional colors can be introduced into the design to create shading. Pour a small amount of Turquoise onto the plastic and mix it with a drop of water to slightly thin the consistency. Dip the small round brush into the paint/water mixture and brush it on the fabric to add shadows and color highlights to the printed design.

Continue to print the entire scarf with designs, unrolling extra fabric as you go. Let it dry completely and heat-set the textile paint according to the bottle instructions.

hints and tips

✿ Do not overapply the paint on the plastic or your fabric will become oversaturated with paint, and you can lose the beauty of the hand-stroke effect.

✿ You can use patterns to create different designs. Just print off the pattern and place it underneath the plastic. Apply paint to the plastic following the pattern lines, then lift and press onto the fabric.

index

patterns

All patterns are shown at actual size.

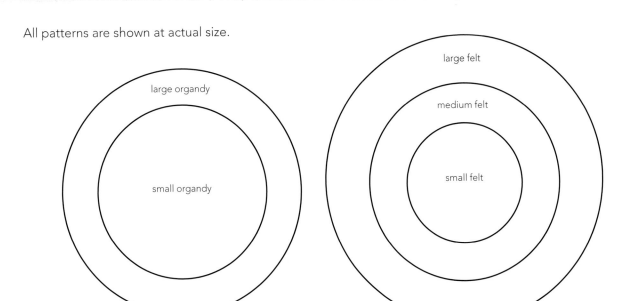

Felt & Organdy Blooms
(circle patterns)

Full of Hearts (heart patterns)

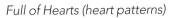

Block-Print Bumblebees
(bee pattern)

18 17 16 15 14   5 4 3 2 1

DISTRIBUTED IN CANADA BY FRASER DIRECT
100 Armstrong Avenue
Georgetown, ON, Canada L7G 5S4
Tel: (905) 877-4411

DISTRIBUTED IN THE U.K. AND EUROPE BY F+W MEDIA INTERNATIONAL
Brunel House, Newton Abbot, Devon, TQ12 4PU, England
Tel: (+44) 1626 323200, Fax: (+44) 1626 323319
Email: enquiries@fwmedia.com

DISTRIBUTED IN AUSTRALIA BY CAPRICORN LINK
P.O. Box 704, S. Windsor NSW, 2756 Australia
Tel: (02) 4560 1600, Fax: (02) 4577 5288
Email: books@capricornlink.com.au

ISBN-13: 978-1-4402-3895-6
ISBN-10: 1-4402-3895-2
SRN: U8344

fw
a content + ecommerce company

Edited by **Stefanie Laufersweiler**
Designed by **Julie Barnett**
Studio photography by **Al Parrish**
Step photography by **Tiffany Windsor**
Illustrations by **Kaysie Schreiner**
Styling by **Lauren Siedentopf**
Production coordinated by **Greg Nock**

resources

Cool2Craft Design Studio
P.O. Box 245
Piru, CA 93040
(626) 616-3113
www.cool2craft.com

Dyes and scarves
Dharma Trading Co.
1604 Fourth St.
San Rafael, CA 94901
Toll-free from anywhere in the USA & Canada:
(800) 542-5227
Everywhere else: (707) 283-0390
www.dharmatrading.com

Merino wool roving
Felt Evolution
105 South Santa Rosa St.
Ventura, CA 93001
(805) 256-0001
www.feltevolution.com

metric conversion chart

TO CONVERT	TO	MULTIPLY BY
inches	centimeters	2.54
centimeters	inches	0.4
feet	centimeters	30.5
centimeters	feet	0.03
yards	meters	0.9
meters	yards	1.1

Projects have been designed and created using imperial measurements and, although metric measurements have been provided, it is important to use either imperial or metric throughout as discrepancies can occur.

about the authors

Tiffany Windsor

Tiffany is best known in the creative community as the founder of the Cool2Craft community, featuring the popular Cool2Craft YouTube web series, and is the host and producer of over 2,000 episodes of craft television programming. Tiffany has made regular appearances on QVC and HSN and has authored numerous hardbound and paperback craft books. Her extensive consulting experience covers all facets of the craft industry including design, product development, manufacturing, retail, publishing, packaging, events, consumer education and more. Tiffany is also an active leader of the Craft and Hobby Association Designer Section and the Southern California CHA Chapter. Visit www.cool2craft.com.

Heidi Borchers

Author of more than 100 paperback and hardbound crafting and lifestyle books, Heidi has created thousands of designs that have been featured in major magazines and on The Learning Channel, Lifetime TV, Hallmark Channel, The Family Channel, The Nashville Network and Cool2Craft. Her innovative and upscale jewelry and gallery art, made from recycled cans and water bottles, have been featured in galleries nationwide. She teaches mosaics and mixed-media art in her California studio. Visit www.heidiborchers.com.

Savannah Starr

A sixth-generation crafter who loves to express her creative style, Savannah has spent countless hours in her grandma Heidi's creative studio. Her style is "Savvy, Sassy and Social," and her passion is to inspire others to use their voices, be kind and move this world forward in a positive manner, aiming to create change. Her creative videos reflect her vivacious, playful and just plain fun personality as she helps to "strike up the creative fire." Visit www.savannahstarr.com.

acknowledgments

We wish to thank our creative brothers and sisters worldwide who share our enthusiasm for creating, and we thank our families, who continue to question the fine line between our hoarding and our growing collections of crafting and creative materials, which fill our studios to the brim. Special thanks to our guest artist and friend Sara Smelt, who has introduced us to a whole new world of artistic expression.

dedication

We dedicate this book to our momma (and Savannah's great-grandma), Aleene, who kicked off the crafting revolution and who has provided generation after generation the inspiration to express their creativity.

Connect • Inspire • Create

Craft It Now
75+ Simple Handmade Projects

Shannon E. Miller

Whether you're craving a new piece of jewelry or an adorable plush bunny, you'll find something to love in *Craft It Now*. The one-of-kind projects from up-and-coming designers have been carefully picked by editor Shannon Miller. With everything from polymer clay to crochet, and cross-stitch to papercraft, this book has you covered when you need a quick craft fix.

Stitch Magazine
Creating With Fabric + Thread

Stitch is the favorite magazine of modern sewists everywhere, featuring vintage modern patterns, embellishment techniques, and modern embroidery designs to name a few. PLUS a full size pattern pullout in every issue. Whether you love bags, clothing, pillows, or other home decor, you are going to love creating the beautiful handmade items you find in *Stitch*. We know you will love every issue.

The Crafter's Book of Clever Ideas
Awesome Craft Techniques for Hand-made Craft Projects

Andrea & Cliff Currie

Andrea and Cliff Currie give you 25 fun projects with his and hers variations for a total of 50 unique gift giving and craft party ideas. Try their clever techniques with a wide range of materials, including glitter, glass, felt and glue gun resin. There's something for every occasion with plenty left over for crafting fun at home.